About the Interpreter's Handbook Series

Signs, Trails, and Wayside Exhibits: Connecting People and Places

The fourth in a series of practical guides for interpretive professionals and students. Other titles in the series are:

Making the Right Connections: A Guide for Nature Writers

The Interpreter's Guidebook: Techniques for Programs and Presentations

Creating Environmental Publications: A Guide to Writing and Designing for Interpreters and Environmental Educators

For more information, contact:

Dr. Michael Gross
College of Natural Resources
University of Wisconsin-Stevens Point
Stevens Point, WI 54481
(715) 346-2076

Cover photo: Schmeeckle Reserve, Wisconsin, by Douglas Moore
Inside cover: Battle Creek Cypress Swamp Sanctuary, Maryland, by Dwight Williams

Suzanne Trapp
U.S. Fish & Wildlife Service
Refuges and Wildlife Support Services
Federal Building
1 Federal Drive
Fort Snelling, MN 55111-4056

Michael Gross
Professor of Environmental Interpretation
College of Natural Resources
University of Wisconsin
Stevens Point, WI 54481

Ron Zimmerman
Director, Schmeeckle Reserve
Instructor of Environmental Interpretation
College of Natural Resources
University of Wisconsin
Stevens Point, WI 54481

Signs, Trails, and Wayside Exhibits
Connecting People and Places

By Suzanne Trapp
Michael Gross and Ron Zimmerman

Tanner Pilley and James Heintzman, Consulting Editors
Line Art by Sylvia Myhre

UW-SP FOUNDATION PRESS, INC.
UNIVERSITY OF WISCONSIN
STEVENS POINT
STEVENS POINT, WI 54481

Signs, Trails, and Wayside Exhibits: Connecting People and Places
Second Edition, 1994

ISBN 0-932310-16-8

Library of Congress Catalog Card Number
91-050427

Printed on
Recycled Paper

Contents

Acknowledgements

The production of this book would not be possible without the assistance of many individuals. We asked for help, advice, and examples. The generous and enthusiastic response from so many people confirmed our perception that this book was needed.

Tanner Pilley of Pilley Associates, Inc. has provided references, photographs, and ideas. Most important was his willingness to share a lifetime of insight gained as a media specialist with the National Park Service. His philosophy and examples are on many pages of this book. We greatly appreciate his editorial review of the final manuscript, helping to fill the gaps, and "turn a better phrase."

Marvin Cook of Wilderness Graphics, Chris Tellis of Antenna, Inc., Ralph Naess of Mount Saint Helens National Volcanic Monument and Debra Erickson of San Diego Wild Animal Park have provided case studies in planning, design, and production. Their contributions provide "practical" insight.

Many people have shared their photograph collections with us. The 270 photographs illustrating this book are some of the finest examples of signs and trails available. Their names appear with their photographs.

A panel of experts on signs and trails generously contributed their time responding to a telephone questionnaire. Many of their insights have been incorporated into the text. Panel members include Marvin Cook of Wilderness Graphics; John Veverka, John Veverka and Associates; Douglas Bruce McHenry of Team Interpretation; Doug Wright of GS Images; Richard Dahn of Dahn Design; Jim Peters of Interpretive Graphic Signs and Systems; Tom Christianson and John Hanna of Inside/Outside; Glen Kaye, Tanner Pilley and Ray Price of the National Park Service.

Special thanks to our consulting editor, James Heintzman. His sensitivity to words improved the readability of this copy.

Finally, we thank Char Pingel who typeset this book, sculpting our ofttimes vague sketches into unified designs. Many extra hours of her creative effort were committed to this final copy.

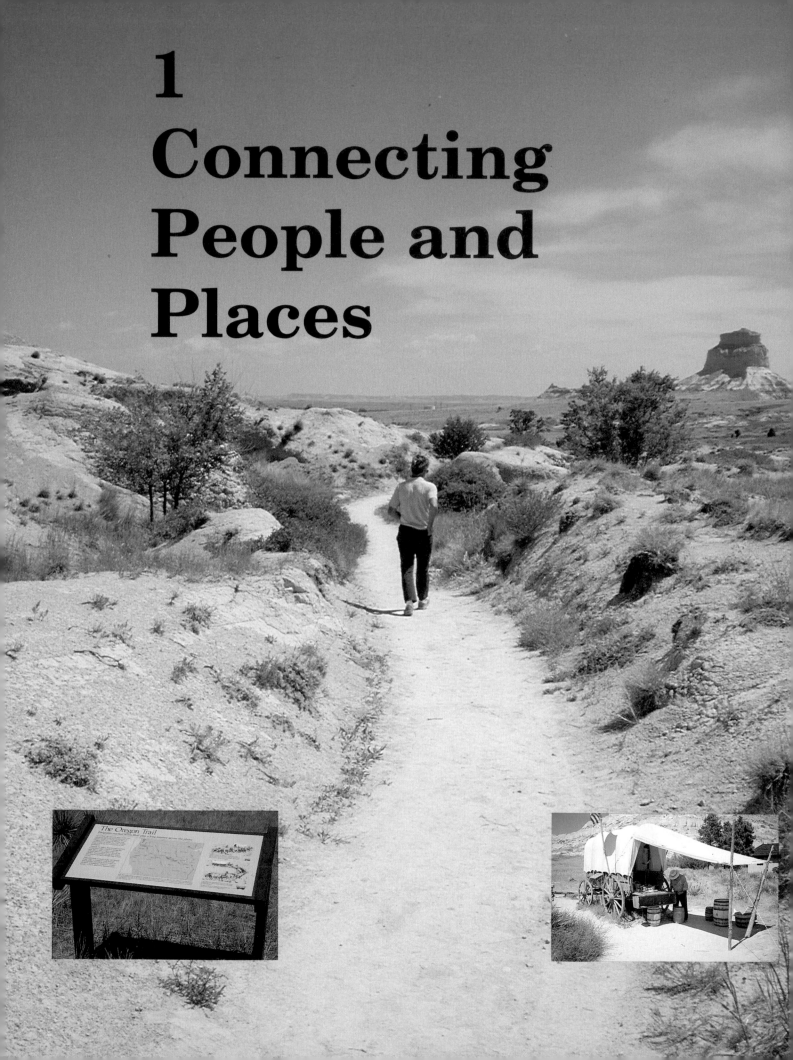

1 Connecting People and Places

A Visitor's Diary

"Scotts Bluff National Monument" on the sign assured me I had arrived. I had been lured to these imposing bluffs by a tiny notation on a highway map.

As I stepped onto the hot pavement, the flapping canvas of a Conestoga wagon beckoned me to investigate. There, an old man, dressed in costume and tinkering with artifacts of a bygone era informed me I was standing on the Oregon Trail.

Walking the trail, the smell of sage and the hum of wind and insects were experiences I shared with pioneer travelers of 140 years ago. Deep ruts were a visible sign of their passing. Who were these people? Why did they come here? What does it mean to me, a 20th century traveler?

Photos by Michael Gross and Ron Zimmerman

As I explored the trail, signs with quotes from diaries and maps and pictures provided answers. I felt a kinship with these fellow travelers whose journeys had ended so long ago.

The Scotts Bluff Experience

Signs, trail panels, and wayside exhibits are connectors. They give meaning to the experience of the moment. At Scotts Bluff, most of the evidences of the passage of the pioneers have been erased by time. The wayside exhibits and trail walk help visualize the passage of people and events when the frontier still lay far to the east.

You are invited to walk the trail and "discover." It is a sensory experience: the sights, smells, and sounds of the plains. It is an intellectual and emotional experience: from the visual impact of the bluff and the pioneer portal at Mitchell Pass, to walking in the physical traces of the trail. The wayside exhibits provide drama and authenticity by quotes from pioneer diaries and through graphic images.

Unity

Unity is the key element in the success of Scotts Bluff National Monument. Thematic unity is achieved through the telling of the story of the pioneers on the Oregon Trail. Living history talks, the museum, and publications are important to expand on this theme, but the trail walks and wayside exhibits link the place to that story.

There is unity in design. Materials and colors are chosen for the entrance sign, building, and wayside exhibits that blend with the landscape. Structures are not imposed on the visitor.

Principles for Success

Scotts Bluff National Monument illustrates several principles for creating effective signs, trail panels, and wayside exhibits.

Signs, trail panels, and wayside exhibits are part of a larger whole.

They are methods for experiencing a site and learning its stories. They seldom provide detailed or in-depth information, but they can provoke visitors to want more. Slide programs, interpreter programs, films, and books provide detail more appropriately to interested visitors.

The site manager must choose media that best meet the needs of visitors at that site. An interpretive plan for the site is needed.

Interpretation should always be based on a unified theme.

What is important about your site? Why has it been set aside? Though you may have many possibilities, choose a theme that reveals the meaning of the site to visitors. Each sign or wayside exhibit should fit into that theme.

Learning is best when it is closely associated with the experience.

Signs, trail panels, and wayside exhibits provide information about real things. Their purpose is to interpret concrete objects and experiences on the site.

Signs, trail panels, and wayside exhibits should be compatible with the site.

They should enhance the on-site experience, not detract from it. Selection of materials, proper placement, and design requires sensitivity and forethought. The worst trail panel or wayside is an irrelevant, undesirable one.

The best interpretation is short and concise.

The urge to add more subject matter may be strong, but must be resisted. Visitors want to experience the site. They will ignore long, complex messages. A good graphic with a short headline may be all that is needed.

As site managers and interpreters, we are custodians of the people's cultural and natural heritage. We are connecting them to their legacy. Signs, trail panels, and wayside exhibits can help make those connections.

2
Sign Basics

Trail Tree, Horicon Marsh, Wisconsin   Donna Zimmerman

Early Signs and Symbols

When Native Americans lashed the limbs of a sapling maple to mark a trail, they left a sign for others crossing the vast Horicon Marsh. Signs have always been a basic form of communication.

Just as Native Americans needed direction across ancient wetlands, today's visitors to natural and cultural sites rely on signs and symbols to find their way. Signs inform, warn, guide, and identify.

Planning for Site Signage

Travelers today are moving fast. Motorists make decisions at a glance. Signs for them must be simple and use letter forms and symbols that communicate quickly. As the visitor's pace slows, signs may become more complex and subtle.

Signs must be deliberately planned to serve all the needs of the visitor as they move through the site. From entrance signs to interpretive signs, each level of signage should be designed to serve a specific purpose.

Jeannie Finley

A **sign** is an inscribed board, plate, or space that provides information, warning, or guidance. Signs provide a single message. Entrance signs, traffic signs, directional signs, and regulation signs are examples.

Reserve du Plaisance, Ottawa   Raymond Tabata

A **wayside exhibit** or **trail panel** interprets features or events on a site to develop a theme or story. It may communicate basic rules and orientation information, but it differs from a sign by providing explanations. The primary purpose is to enhance the visitor's experience and understanding. These are designed for learning at leisure.

Anatomy of a Sign

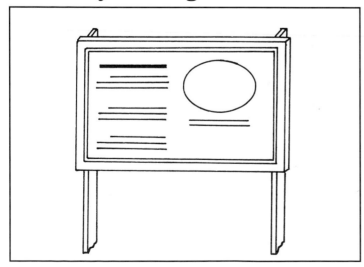

Each part of a sign or wayside exhibit is important. Signs not only provide information, they create an impression and set a tone. Three parts of a sign are:

sign face - includes all the elements that compose the surface.

sign panel - the physical backboard or which the sign face is inscribed.

supports - anchor the sign to the site physically and visually.

Sign Faces

Sign Face Components

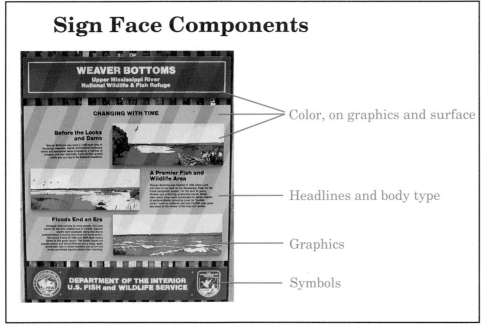

Upper Mississippi River National Wildlife Refuge

Color, on graphics and surface

Headlines and body type

Graphics

Symbols

Henry Schneider

A sign face greets the visitor and expresses a personality. It is the surface to which is applied the cosmetics of color, type, graphics, and symbols for maximum effect.

The Fraction of Selection

Why do people choose to read or ignore a sign? Signs that provoke interest and are simple and inviting will be selected by more people.

The success of a sign can be viewed as a formula, proposed by Wilbur Shramm as The Fraction of Selection:

The Fraction = $\dfrac{\text{Expectation of Reward}}{\textbf{Effort Required}}$
of Selection
(low)

The Fraction = $\dfrac{\textbf{Expectation of Reward}}{\text{Effort Required}}$
of Selection
(high)

To be successful in creating signs, your challenge is to increase the expectation of reward and decrease the effort required. The fraction of selection is a result of how you craft your message and how you design your sign. Tips for improving inscriptions are in Chapter 4. Tips for design follow.

Badlands National Park, South Dakota

Michael Gross

Selecting a Typeface

Choosing and placing type on your sign face should not be left to chance. Each typestyle speaks its own language. John Downy, an Iowa artist and signmaker states, "The letters on a sign should demand to be noticed. They need to aggressively catch the eye and hold attention."

Downy provides a rule for text designers: "If a reader says in the process of reading a book, 'Hey, I don't think I've seen this typeface before!' then it is probably a bad typeface. And, if a person can walk by a sign without becoming a reader, it's probably a bad sign."

You don't have to become a master of typography to create effective signs. You just need to learn the basic principles for choosing a typeface and the spacing and sizing of letters.

Font Styles for Signs

Times (abcdefghijklmnopqrstuvwxyz)
Times is a good serif style for signs.

Helvetica (abcdefghijklmnopqrstuvwxyz)
Helvetica is a sans serif style that has good readability.

Improving legibility with fonts:
- *Avoid script and fancy fonts. Letters are hard to distinguish from one another.*
- Try not to mix font styles. It creates disharmony. Instead use *italics,* **bold**, and print size variations for emphasis.

Each typeface has its unique personality. Typeface selection handbooks are available in libraries and from local printers. Select a face that expresses the personality you desire.

Serif vs. Sans Serif

Apostle Islands National Lakeshore, Wisconsin   Michael Gross

The National Park Service developed a serif typeface for many of its signs that says "parks are places for leisurely activity, not speedways." (A serif is a bar that crosses letter ends.)

Big Cypress National Preserve, Florida   Michael Gross

Highway signs with sans serif typefaces can be read rapidly. This is a cool, modern typeface that conveys little emotion.

Proportion and Size of Lettering

Recommended Type Sizes

Vertical Measurement	Viewing Distance
1/2"	4'
5/8"	6'
2 1/2"	30'
4"	60'

or

Titles - 72 to 60 point minimum
Subtitles - 48 to 40 point minimum
Body text - 24 point minimum
Captions - 18 point minimum

(Complies with suggested sizes for visually impaired as per National Park Service recommendations.)

The High Life

Ancient Sinagua farmers weren't the only creatures to seek out the ledges and caves in these limestone cliffs for homes. Watch for the movements—and listen for the sounds—of a surprising variety of cliffside animal neighbors.

Canyon wrens . . . spend all year round high in the cliffs. Listen for their descending trills.

Cliffside swallows . . . return each spring to raise their young in mud nests stuck to cliff overhangs. Watch their acrobatic swoopings as they search out meals of insects.

Rock squirrels . . . play and sun themselves on even the most precarious ledges.

Montezuma Castle National Monument, Arizona   Tanner Pilley

There is a hierarchy of letter sizes on this sign. Their size suggests the order in which the message should be read. They are proportional to each other and to the sign as a whole.

Letter Spacing

Letters should be aligned with the eye, not mechanical lines. Variations in the weight and shape of letters will make some appear more widely spaced than others. Others will seem closer together. When laying letters on a sign face, adjust them optically to appear equal in distance.

Mechanically spaced:

HILLY ACRES

Poor arrangement.

Optically spaced:

HILLY ACRES

Better arrangement.

Ragged Right vs. Justified

This paragraph has right margins that are set ragged. All other text is justified, i.e., flush right and left. Generally, text for signs should be set flush left and ragged right. This improves reading ease and allows for uniform letter spacing. It is also less formal.

Use of Caps

Florida   Michael Gross

Large blocks of type set in caps are difficult to read. A sign set in all caps takes 14 percent longer to read and takes up 40 percent more space.

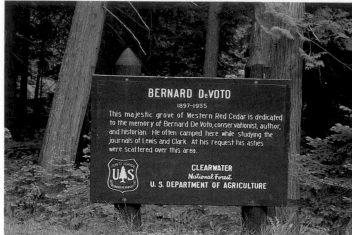

Idaho   Michael Gross

Caps on this sign are limited to headlines. It is more readable.

Open Space

Missouri   Michael Gross

In addition to using all caps, the type crowds the sign face. When words are crowded into a tight space, there is no room for the eye to relax. People won't read a crowded text.

Utah   Michael Gross

When text "has room to breathe," it is more inviting. This sign has more open space on its margins.

Symbols and Graphics

Communicate through the universal language of symbols. Symbols and objects are more identifiable than words. Even a young child can recognize the Golden Arches of a McDonald's restaurant or the familiar face of Smokey the Bear.

Visual images may be the only communication with non-reading or foreign visitors. A large segment of our population cannot read and we need to accommodate them.

The Federal Graphics Improvement Program for the Department of Interior developed this set of symbols to convey essential messages.

General

Area where deer might be viewed by visitors.

A light house.

Visitor information.

Drinking water.

Recreation

Cross-country ski trail.

Interpretive trail.

Hiking trail.

Area where swimming permitted.

Accommodations or Service

Area where public camping permitted.

Restrooms for men and women.

Picnic shelter.

Area where campfires permitted.

For a complete set of symbols, refer to *Code of Federal Regulations, Parks, Forests, and Public Property,* Volume 36, Parts 1-199, revised July 1, 1989.

Graphics

Graphics on interpretive signs convey detailed stories in concise and dramatic ways. A single graphic image can replace many words. They can also focus attention and lead the eye through a message sequence. Graphics also add beauty and interest to a sign face. Graphic images have more impact than words.

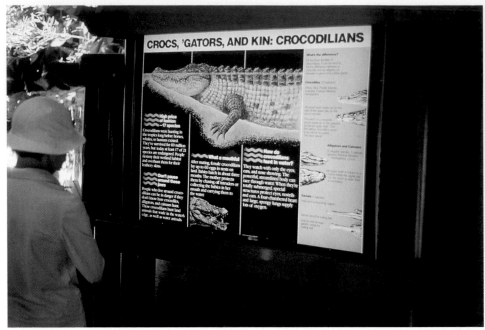

Miami Metro Zoo   Paul Trapp

Awkland, New Zealand   Raymond Tabata

Alaska   Chuck Lennox

Sign Panels

Sign panels can be created from many materials including metal, fiberglass, wood, concrete, and plastic. These materials can be made attractive and vibrant by variations of color, illumination, texture, and shape. Durability and aesthetics are the two main criteria for panel selection.

Sanibel Island, Florida   Michael Gross

Wood

Best Uses:
Where rustic, natural appearance is important.

Options:
Sandblasted, carved, routed.

Advantages:
Natural - blends with landscape.
Three-dimensional, can be shaped and carved.
Each sign is different.
Ages gracefully.
Convey endurance, permanence as they weather.
Absorb gunshot.
More easily constructed and repaired in-house.

Disadvantages:
More construction effort.
Copies require equal effort.
Easily carved by vandals.
Detailed graphics more difficult and less durable.

Fiberglass Embedment

Best Uses:
Where detailed graphics are needed, such as wayside exhibits and trail interpretation.
Are very cost effective for directional or rules signs where many duplicates are needed.

Advantages:
Durable. Resistant to weather and vandalism.
Copies easily made.
Graphic detail.
Wide range of colors.
Can embed photographs directly (no half toning or color separation).

Disadvantages:
Doesn't accept photos well.
Color subject to fading and yellowing.
Requires framing and backing.
Easily scratched, but can be buffed out with car wax.

Cape Perpetua Scenic Area, Oregon   Dahn Design

Metal

Fort Hartsuff, Nebraska   Michael Gross

Cast metal at a memorial to a Nebraska fort.

Best Uses:
Memorials - cast metal.
Road signs - painted metal.
Small trail markers - etched or anodized.

Options:
Painted surface (often silk-screened).
Cast aluminum or iron.
Etched or engraved.
Anodized.

Advantages:
Does not require framing or backing.
Durability - resistant to weather and most vandalism.

Disadvantages:
Some metals subject to rusting.
Thin metals subject to gunshot.
Usually expensive.
Costs of duplicates usually remains high.
Some choices "glare" in bright sun.

Metal-Micro Imaging

Best Uses:
Historical interpretation.
Commemorative plaques.
Trail markers.
Wayside exhibits.

Advantages:
Very durable, even in extreme environmental conditions.
Requires no framing.
Vandal resistant.
Reproduces black and white photos and line art well.
Combinations of bronze, gold, silver, blue, black, red, and green are available, but limited to two colors per sign.

Disadvantages:
Limited to line art, black and white photos, and two colors per sign.
Multiple copies don't significantly reduce cost.

Saguaro National Monument, Arizona   Tanner Pilley

Porcelain Enamel

Best Uses:
Where colorful and detailed graphics are needed as in zoos and other high use areas.

Advantages:
Ability to reproduce high resolution photographs and fine line art.
Vivid colors that do not fade.
Little maintenance required.
Equal or greater vandal resistance than other mediums.
Impervious to all natural elements.

Disadvantages:
Slightly more expensive than other mediums.
Requires framing or backing.
Can chip and then rust

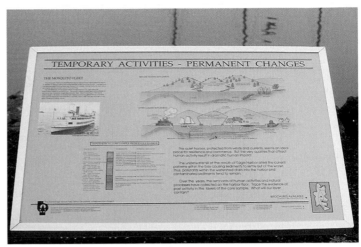

Bainbridge Island, Washington   The Porcelain Company

Comparing Three Panel Materials

Porcelain Enamel

Metal Micro-imaged

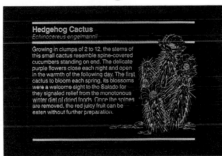

Fiberglass Embedment

Courtesy of Pilley Associates

The same sign has been made in three different materials. There are slight cost differences in the three mediums that will vary depending on graphics and design. The interpreter is encouraged to consider factors besides cost when selecting interpretive materials.

Panel Tips

- **Inexpensive materials in large rectangles, such as a 4' x 8' sheet of plywood, should be avoided. This creates a billboard appearance.**

- **Avoid square panels. A 5 to 3 or 5 to 4 ratio is more visually appealing.**

- **Use panel materials that are appropriate to your site. Avoid highly reflective materials that create glare. Choose materials that are insect, salt, and water resistant.**

- **Select panel materials based on:**
  long term maintenance requirements/vandalism risk.
  budget limitations or cost/benefit.
  color and graphic needs.

Other Panel Materials

Miami Metro Zoo   Suzanne Trapp

The Miami Metro Zoo sign combines ceramic cast relief figures and plastic inscription panels mounted on wood.

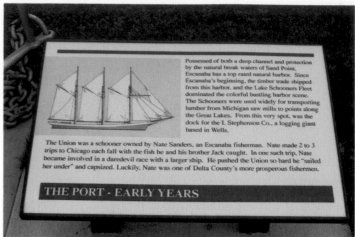

Municipal Dock, Escanaba, Michigan   Courtesy of Genesis Graphics

Lexan-aluminum laminate is an inexpensive alternative to fiberglass embedment. A reverse image is silk screened onto a clear durable plastic (Lexan) and backed with enameled aluminum. Field tests at the Hiawatha National Forest in northern Michigan have proven its durability. See Resources, page 107, for source.

Los Angeles, California   Michael Gross

Nevada   Ron Zimmerman

Colorado   Michael Gross

Medium Density Overlay (MDO) (right) is an inexpensive alternative for wayside and trail panels. Text and graphics are silk screened over painted enamel. MDO plywood is available through any lumber company. It can be made by local sign shops, and duplicates can be produced for moderate additional expense. Although environmentally durable, it is less vandal resistant than other panel materials. Other examples are the Madison Buffalo Jump signs (page 31).

Cast concrete is durable and blends well with some sites (top left).
Concrete and iron resists damage from ORV's (middle left).
Cast fiberglass has the appearance of carved wood, but requires less maintenance (bottom left).

Upper Missippi River National
Wildlife and Fish Refuge   Henry A. Schneider

Sign Supports

Supports do more than hold up the sign. They can also imply permanence and respect for a site and provide a link with site features.

Supports are esthetically pleasing only when they relate to their purpose and surroundings. Real charm is a result of creativeness, imagination, and sensitivity to the site.

The physical quality of supports should have a harmonious relationship with the natural environment, buildings, or the site theme.

Tatra Mountain Nat. Park, Poland   Michael Gross
This trail closed sign in Tatra Mountain National Park, Poland, uses carefully chosen natural timbers.

Hawaii Volcanoes National Park   Donna Zimmerman
Native materials are often used to mirror the site features.

Mount Rushmore, South Dakota   Suzanne Trapp
Colors and materials can be selected to complement the site.

Hans Sutter Wildlife Area, Texas   Michael Gross
Supports may be more visual than physical. These heavy timbers were needed to visually balance the heavy sign face.

Zion National Park, Utah   Ron Zimmerman

Color and landforms are reflected in this entrance sign.

Padre Island National Lakeshore, Texas

Michael Gross

The sand dunes of Padre Island are suggested in this support.

Corkscrew Swamp Audubon Sanctuary, Florida   Michael Gross

Natural supports and plantings are a way to frame signs in nature preserves.

Cape Pepetua Scenic Area, Oregon   Dahn Design

Vertical timbers repeat the tree patterns. Their boldness emphasizes this wayside's significance.

Aransas National Wildlife Refuge   Michael Gross

Symbolic supports are used to set expectations.

Nez Perce National Historical Park, ID Michael Gross

Boise, Idaho   Dahn Design

A rock formation can be an effective support.

A roof over a bulletin board or wayside exhibit draws the visitor into the shelter of the overhang. It creates a defined space where people feel protected.

Bulletin board at Denali Park, Alaska

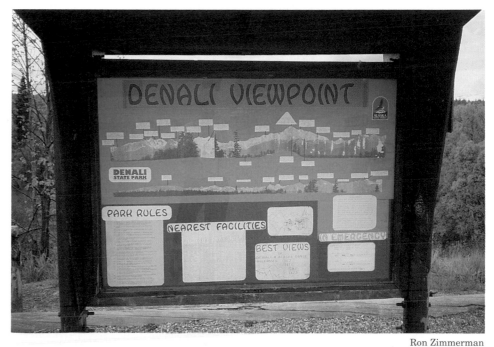

Ron Zimmerman

The shelter invites you to leave your car and study the information provided. It also protects the materials from the elements.

Moody Air Force Base, Georgia · Wilderness Graphics

Padre Island National Seashore, TX · Michael Gross

A roof over a trailhead and orientation sign is an invitation to stop before starting on the trail.

Design Fundamentals

Design is the organization of the visual elements of a sign. Every good sign has a focal point, movement, balance, unity, and proportion in varying degrees. Design can be largely intuitive, but a pleasing visual image follows certain principles.

Visual Flow Through a Sign

This logo leads the eye clockwise through the title and symbols of the park.

Sea Life Park, California   Donna Zimmerman

When a circular logo serves as a focal point, a "break," such as this hawk, can lead the eye out of the circle and into a title.

Schmeeckle Reserve, Wisconsin   Ron Zimmerman

Sitka National Historic Park, Alaska   Chuck Lennox

In addition to graphics, letter sizes dictate the eyes' direction of travel. Larger letters are read first.

Glacier National Park, Montana   Michael Gross

"Living creatures" on signs should usually be moving into the text. Notice that the antler connects with the title. Breaking lines create eye focusing tension. The moose captures the eye and the antlers lead into the title.

Missouri Department of Conservation

The converging lines of this illustration and title guide the eye.

Balance and Unity

Acadia National Park, Maine   Michael Gross

Squares or combinations of squares should be avoided. This panel has been divided into thirds and mounted asymmetrically to add to the visual interest. Visual divisions into thirds are preferable to halves. Formal symmetry is balanced, at rest. Asymmetry is dynamic.

Aransas National Wildlife Refuge, Texas   Michael Gross

Spaces arranged in halves are less compelling. Neither side of the panel demands your attention. Larger headings, layered text, or converging lines within the graphics would provoke more interest. If both spaces are equal, it implies everything is equally important, with no focus.

Whitefish Point Lighthouse, Michigan   Michael Gross

Borders, or in this case a rope, can frame and unify loose elements of a sign face. The maritime motif connects the sign and the site.

Lines

Schmeeckle Reserve, Wisconsin   Ron Zimmerman

Vertical lines imply power. Vertical supports blend with a forest environment.

Gray's Lake National Wildlife Refuge, Idaho   Wilderness Graphics

Horizontal lines generally convey peacefulness. Long low signs fit well in a marsh setting.

An overlook at the end of a short climb provides visitors with information on whooping cranes and a spotting scope to assist in viewing birds.

Color

Color provides variety, emphasis, and unity along with the illusion of depth. It can evoke a mood and complement the theme or landscape.

Schmeeckle Reserve, Wisconsin

The bright background in this logo captures your attention. The yellow border unifies the elements. Yellow letters on a brown background create contrast and emphasis.

Schmeeckle Reserve, Wisconsin

These bright yellow and orange letters are exciting and active, fitting the trail's purpose. Warm letters on a dark background "advance" toward a viewer, giving a three-dimensional quality to the sign.

Glacier National Park, Montana   Michael Gross

This strong color contrast emphasizes the message.

Color unifies and organizes this complex wayside exhibit.

Alaska Pipeline   Chuck Lennox

Mount Saint Helens National Volcanic Monument, Washington   Michael Gross

The mood of this sign is introverted and passive. Value contrasts are minimal, gray predominates, and the opposing maroon lettering is relatively neutral. It effectively complements the landscape.

Schmeeckle Reserve, Wisconsin   Michael Gross

A splash of color on a neutral background commands attention.

Mosquito Hill Nature Center, Wisconsin   Jim Anderson

Sometimes the natural beauty of wood and a small amount of color is best.

Blue Springs State Park, Florida   Michael Gross

Light-colored backgrounds with dark letters are more readable in shaded areas.

Badlands National Park, South Dakota   Michael Gross

Dark signs with light letters are easier to read in bright sun.

Design Checklist

- **Keep the sign face simple and uncluttered.**

- **Maintain open space, especially on margins.**

- **Have a strong center of interest or focal point.**

- **Develop a visual sequence from the focal point. Do this through graphics and varying message levels.**

- **Connect all signs to each other and to their environment.**

- **Create short readable messages.**

- **Choose readable typefaces.**

- **Use a minimum of CAPITAL letters.**

- **Use symbols and graphics, not just words.**

3
Wayside Exhibits

Turnagain Arm, Alaska   Ron Zimmerman

Beluga Point wayside invites travelers on Alaska's Seward Highway to learn about this spectacular area. Even the name promises adventure. Beluga whales are featured since they are often seen feeding off this point. Other panels tell about tidal bores and Captain Cook's voyage up Turnagain Arm.

This wayside exhibit endures frequent storms to greet new visitors. Through long summer days, it tells the story of Turnagain Arm. This wayside is filled with information about the cultural and natural history around it. Visitors take as much or as little as they want. The exhibit receives no overtime pay, takes no vacations, and requires no supervision.

Beluga Point is a good place for a wayside exhibit because:

• There are events or features here which demand explanation. How did it get the name Turnagain Arm?

• Thousands of visitors would miss seeing the belugas if the whales were not brought to their attention. How else would they know that this was a stop on Captain Cook's voyage?

• It is a safe and convenient place for drivers to stop. The avalanches common at Turnagain Arm are not a threat here. The wayside is visible at a distance so motorists have time to stop.

Turnagain Arm, Alaska

Ron Zimmerman

When to Use a Wayside Exhibit

• **When it is the best media for a story. Would a roving interpreter or a publication be better? Are those and other options available?**

• **When there are features or events that need explanation. Would a visitor have questions that would otherwise go unanswered?**

• **When there are enough visitors to justify the expense of a wayside exhibit.**

• **When a wayside exhibit does not detract from the site or invite people into a site too sensitive for public use.**

• **When it is a safe and convenient place for people to stop.**

Wayside Examples

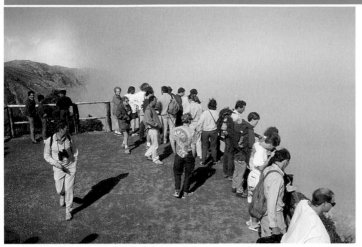

Poas Volcano National Park, Costa Rica
Wayside exhibits should be placed wherever visitors congregate and ask questions.

Donna Zimmerman
They can be as simple as a single interpretive sign.

Sometimes a story requires more than a single sign. Madison Buffalo Jump is a destination for travelers on Interstate 90. It takes effort to get there, but travelers are rewarded with interesting stories told through a series of panels.

Madison Buffalo Jump State Monument, Montana

Michael Gross

A traditional Nez Perce design is used for this shelter. It houses panels telling the story of White Bird's battle with federal troops. Visitors are offered panoramic views of the battlefield.

Nez Perce National Historical Park, Idaho

Michael Gross

Grey Cliff Prairie Dog State Monument, Montana
Photos by Michael Gross

Prairie dogs are a popular attraction for travelers on Interstate 90. The Grey Cliff wayside uses metal micro-imaged panels to explain the life history of the prairie dog.

Objects Connect Visitors to the Story

Fort Sumpter, South Carolina   Paul Trapp

A cannon is a tangible artifact of the Civil War.

Mt. Saint Helens National Volcanic Preserve, Washington   Michael Gross

A crushed car shows the power of the volcanic eruption at Mount Saint Helens. The fence protects it from souvenir hunters. Its presence provokes questions that a wayside exhibit can answer.

Chuck Lennox

A Tlingit canoe brings life to the interpretation of an intriguing culture. The canopy protects it from heavy rainfall.

Glacier Bay National Park, Alaska   Chuck Lennox

A replica of a log raft brings the past to life. Old photographs on the sign help tell the story.

Black Forest, Germany   Michael Gross

Topical and Temporary Themes

Foresters in the Black Forest of Germany created a wayside exhibit to provoke concern about the effects of acid rain on the forest. It includes informational panels and trees marked to show the progressive decline caused by airborne pollutants.

Black Forest, Germany

Michael Gross

Visitors to the San Diego Wild Animal Park are prepared to spend the day. Wayside exhibits are used to develop sub-themes for them.

The xeriscape garden exhibit tells why native vegetation should be used to landscape yards in arid climates.

San Diego Wild Animal Park, California

Michael Gross

Seasonal panels can interpret ephemeral events. Visitors to this wetland learn the spring songs of breeding frogs.

Schmeeckle Reserve, Wisconsin

Audio Exhibits

An audio message requires no reading, communicates more information than signs, and is easily changed. It can also involve visitors' emotions. See Resources, page 108, for sources of digital sound units.

Custer Battlefield National Monument, Montana

Michael Gross

An audio message describes the final moments of George Custer's 7th calvary.

Production Tips for Audio Messages

- **Keep it short. Three minutes is more than enough in most situations.**

- **The feel of a production should always be live rather than canned. Don't sound like you are reading from a script. Use the first person and second person where possible.**

- **Pretest your scripts for pacing and comprehension before recording.**

- **Use sound effects. Natural sounds and sound effects set a mood for the message.**

- **Use voices in dialect. When used appropriately, they transport the visitor back in time and place.**

- **Use professional production studios, but make your interpretive themes and wishes clear to them. Local radio stations and private studios can help you produce high quality taped messages.**

- **Use digital sound equipment to insure durability.**

4
The Message

Except for the rare instances of inspiration, I should guess that the adequate interpretive inscription will be the result of ninety percent thinking and ten percent composition. Inspiration is usually the mirrored reflection of hard work.

Freeman Tilden
Interpreting Our Heritage

Developing an Effective Message

Seven Ways to an Effective Message

- Say it visually. Use photos and drawings to help tell the story.

- Graphics should do more than duplicate what can be seen. They should reveal hidden meanings and ideas.

- Use a message pyramid: develop a descending order of message importance. This can be expressed as the 3-30-3 rule. Visitors can receive a message in three seconds, thirty seconds, or three minutes.

- Keep the message short! Use short sentences, short paragraphs. Use a readability scale such as the Flesch test to help eliminate wordy phrases and paragraphs. (See Resources for Flesch Readability Test.)

- Use concrete nouns and active verbs.

- Relate to the visitor's experience. Use personal pronouns, personal language, and familiar terms.

- Illustrate with metaphors, analogies, quotes, and real examples.

Interpretive signs compete for the visitor's attention with warm sunshine, cold rains, and colorful birds. They are static objects in a dynamic environment.

To be effective, an interpretive sign must communicate quickly and dramatically. The message must be important to the visitor and relate to what they can see or experience.

The visitor must feel that reading this sign is worth the effort. Too much effort for no apparent reward means the message will be ignored.

The following examples show how these seven principles can be used to improve a message. These examples were selected from sites in our National Park and National Wildlife Refuge systems.

Example 1 - Original Sign and Message

MANY PARKS CURVE

THE IMPRINT OF ICE. MUCH OF THE SURROUNDING SCENERY WAS SHAPED BY GLACIAL ICE OVER 15,000 YEARS AGO. DURING THAT TIME, THE COLD CLIMATE ALLOWED GLACIERS TO FORM IN MOUNTAIN RECESSES HIGH ABOVE. EVENTUALLY, ALL OF THE MAJOR CANYONS IN AND AROUND ROCKY MOUNTAIN NATIONAL PARK WERE FILLED WITH TONS OF ICE, SOME TO A DEPTH OF 1,500 FEET. AS THESE FROZEN TRIBUTARIES DESCENDED TO LOWER ELEVATIONS, THEY SCOURED AND POLISHED THE LANDSCAPE, CREATING THE STRIATED SLOPES AND U-SHAPED CANYONS.

IN THE VALLEYS BELOW, GLACIERS FORMED A MASSIVE PLUG 200 FEET THICK AND MORE THAN EIGHT MILES LONG. THESE ICY GIANTS DOMINATED THE SCENE UNTIL APPROXIMATELY 13,000 TO 14,000 YEARS AGO, WHEN A WARMING CLIMATE CAUSED THE GLACIERS TO BEGIN THEIR RETREAT. VAST QUANTITIES OF DERIS RELEASED BY MELTING ICE FORMED HUGE MOUNDS CALLED MORAINES. IN MORAINE PARK, THESE FEATURES APPEAR AS LONG, TREE-COVERED RIDGES.

THOUGH THE ANCIENT GLACIERS HAVE LONG-SINCE WASTED AWAY, IMPRINTS OF THEIR PASSING REMAIN AS SOME OF THE MOST SPECTACULAR SCENERY IN NORTH AMERICA.

ABOUT GLACIERS. GLACIERS BEGIN AS SNOW FIELDS HIGH ABOVE THE THAW LINE. AS THESE SNOW FIELDS BECOME DEEPER, THEY COMPACT INTO GRANDEUR MASSES OF ICE. GRADUALLY THESE FIELDS THICKEN UNTIL THEIR OWN INTERNAL WEIGHT, COMBINED WITH GRAVITY, CAUSE THEM TO FLOW AS GLACIERS.

GLACIERS SHAPED THE LANDSCAPE BY PLUCKING, SHEARING, AND COMPRESSING AS THEY MORE. MOVEMENT INSIDE THE ICE MASS IS ALWAYS FORWARD, SO THE COLLECTED DEBRIS IS ALWAYS CARRIED TOWARD THE FRONT, ADDING TO THE GLACIERS ABRASIVE POWER.

THOUGH GLACIERS MAY LAST FOR THOUSANDS OF YEARS, THE ICE MAY BE ONLY HUNDREDS OF YEARS OLD. THE ICE, CONSTANTLY BEING REPLENISHED FROM ABOVE, LASTS AS LONG AS IT TAKES TO MOVE FROM THE CIRQUE TO THE FRONT OF THE GLACIER. IT CRAWLS FROM SEVERAL INCHES TO SEVERAL FEET PER DAY.

WHEN GLACIERS RECEDE FASTER THAN THEY ADVANCE, THEY RELEASE A VAST AMOUNT OF ROCK, SAND, AND OTHER DEBRIS WHICH WAS PICKED UP ALONG THE WAY. WHEN LEFT IN ELONGATED PILES, THIS MATERIAL FORMS THE LATERAL AND END MORAINES, THE LATTER MARKING THE FARTHEST POINT REACHED BY THE ICE FIELD.

Recommendations for Change

Implied Purpose: To illustrate to the visitor how glaciers changed the landscape.

Recommendations:
- Shorten and simplify message.
- Use vivid language.
- Create a message pyramid.
- Change capital letters to lower case.
- Integrate graphic and message.
- Set text ragged right.

(revised text)   **The Imprint of Ice**

Glaciers carved these mountains and valleys more than 15,000 years ago.

Snow accumulated in high, shaded valleys until it was compressed into flowing ice. Glaciers surged to life, bulldozing and scouring the valleys.

Warmer summers shrank the glaciers back to the high snowfields we see today.

Bowl-shaped depressions, called cirques, mark places where glaciers are born.

U-shaped valleys are remnants of a glacier's passage.

Moraines are lines of debris dropped when the glaciers melted.

New Reading Ease Score = 73, Fairly Easy

Redesign courtesy of Wilderness Graphics, Inc.

Example 2 - Original Sign and Message

EVALUATION

Flesch Reading Ease Score: 56, Fairly Difficult

Assessment of Problems:
- Text copied from an agency publication and not written for a sign inscription. As a result, it is not succinct.
- The visitor is not actively engaged in the message.
- Graphic is weak and does not amplify the message.

Visitor Appeal: Low.
Graphic and text do not promise reward to the visitor.

Freshwater Marsh

The natural values of freshwater marshes have just begun to be understood. An obvious value is their importance to wildlife. The nightly chorus of frogs and toads reflect their abundance. Salamanders congregate to lay eggs. Newly spawned sunfish, bass, and bullheads hide among the plants. Songbirds, shorebirds, and waterfowl raise their young among the reeds and cattails. Marshes provide important habitat for migrating birds, as well as deer, raccoon, bobcat, muskrat, and mink.

Alligators are a prominent part of the wildlife in these marshes. Alligators often dig large holes which serve as reservoirs during dry periods. Thus, "gator" holes provide the source for renewal of life when the marsh is flooded again.

Freshwater marshes provide floodwater storage, wastewater storage, and groundwater recharging. They are, indeed, a most valuable part of our natural resources.

Recommendations for Change

Implied Purpose: To communicate the value and diversity of a freshwater marsh.

Recommendations:
- Write message for someone who is sitting in a car, on-site.
- Shorten and simplify message.
- Use vivid language.
- Create a message pyramid.
- Use a graphic that simplifies and organizes the message.

(revised text)   **Reservoirs of Life**

This marsh is a living sponge. It filters and purifies water. It is home to a diverse abundance of plants and animals.

What Does a Marsh Do for You?

The marsh stores water and slowly releases it to the groundwater. Marsh plants filter pollutants from your drinking water. They protect from floods by slowing the runoff of rainwater. Marshes are truly reservoirs of life for all creatures, including us.

Gator Holes -

During dry seasons, depressions dug by "gators" store water. Many creatures survive drought in these dangerous "refuges." A few will be eaten by the resident gator.

New Reading Ease Score = 70, Fairly Easy

Redesign courtesy of Wilderness Graphics, Inc.

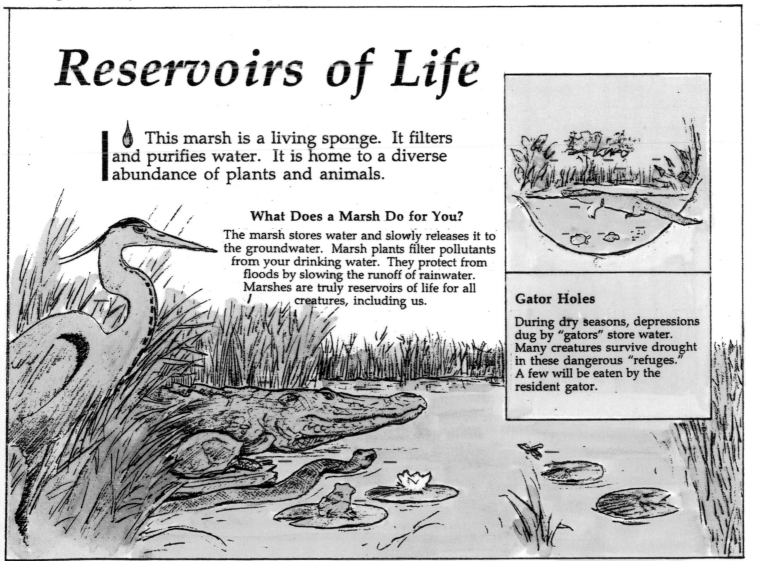

Reservoirs of Life

This marsh is a living sponge. It filters and purifies water. It is home to a diverse abundance of plants and animals.

What Does a Marsh Do for You?
The marsh stores water and slowly releases it to the groundwater. Marsh plants filter pollutants from your drinking water. They protect from floods by slowing the runoff of rainwater. Marshes are truly reservoirs of life for all creatures, including us.

Gator Holes
During dry seasons, depressions dug by "gators" store water. Many creatures survive drought in these dangerous "refuges." A few will be eaten by the resident gator.

Example 3 - Original Sign and Message

THE FRAGILE TUNDRA

The alpine tundra ecosystems were in dynamic equilibrium with the Native Americans who left evidence of their thousands of years of presence in the "Ute Trail." In the late 1800's, the heavier tread of meat hunters' and miners' boots and of horses hooves deepened the trail which crossed the continental divide and went the length of "Trail Ridge." Change brought Trail Ridge Road, which followed the old route, in 1932, and the beginning of a great influx of visitors. Evidence of man then became much more evident in the fragile tundra. This study plot was established in 1959. It is assisting in finding out about alpine vegetation recovery from the trampling of visitor's feet. About five million feet visit the park each year. Some of those feet concentrated on tundra for a summer, as here, can make impacts that can take a decade or more to recover. You can help by staying on established trails. Or when hiking across country, by stepping from rock to rock.

Recommendations for Change

Implied Purpose: To demonstrate to visitors the effect they have on the tundra.

Recommendations:
- Create a message pyramid.
- Simplify and shorten message.
- Reduce length of sentences.
- Use vivid, active language.
- Replace photos with line drawings to better illustrate the message and to create a visual flow.
- Reset type to more readable line length and layout.

(revised text)   **The Trampled Tundra**

This plot has been protected since 1959. It is testimony to the slow recovery of the tundra from the trample of human feet.

The occasional moccasin on the old Ute Trail had little impact. In the 1800's, boots of miners and hunters and the hooves of their horses cut the tundra into ribbons of trails. Trail Ridge Road opened in 1932 to caravans of tourists. Five million feet now visit the park each year.

Help heal the tundra. Stay on marked trails or step from rock to rock when hiking cross-country.

New Reading Ease Score: 79, Fairly Easy

Redesign courtesy of Wilderness Graphics, Inc.

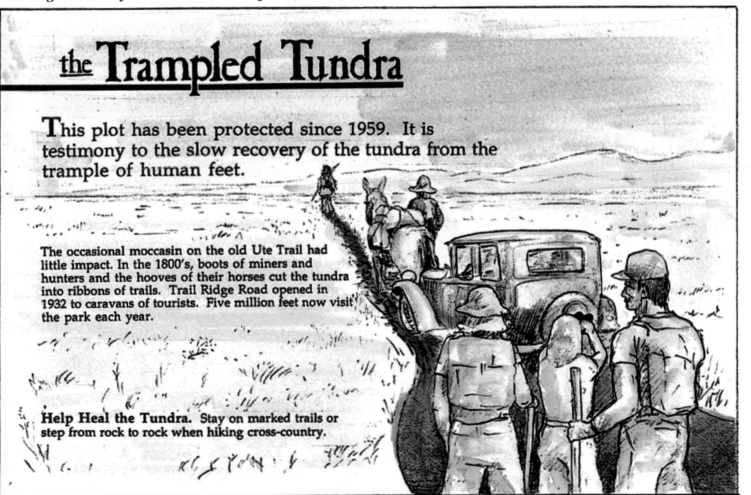

Beyond Prose

Like poetry and paintings, a sign message should inspire and provoke in bold and simple language. It is an art form of the essence. The quantity of words is often inversely proportional to the success of a sign. Strive for fresh perspectives, poetic twists, vivid imagery, and simple eloquence.

The challenge of the inscription writer is to involve the reader intellectually, emotionally, or physically. The message should help the visitor see the site in a new way.

Take time to see the sky
Find shapes in the clouds
Hear the murmur of the wind
And touch the cool water.
Walk softly—
We are the intruders
Tolerated briefly
In an infinite universe.

Montezuma Castle National Monument, Arizona   Tanner Pilley

A sign like this one greeted wilderness campers at the Philmont Scout Ranch in the 1960's. Detailed explanation is not always good communication. Monument to a Careless Camper actively provokes the reader to ponder meaning beyond the words.

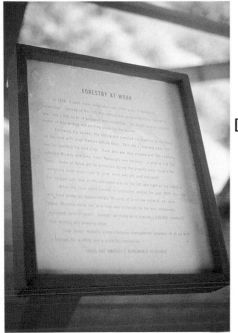

Industrial forest site, Wisconsin

FORESTRY AT WORK

In 1974, a sleet storm devastated over 7,000 acres of Nekoosa's timberland. Salvage of this 155 acre setting was accomplished the following year and 2,300 cords of pulpwood were harvested. That would provide 460,000 reams of fine writing and printing paper for the market.

Following the harvest, the setting was prepared for planting by churning up the land with large tractors pulling discs. This left a relatively clean seedbed for planting the next crop. Each acre was then planted with 900 carefully selected Norway red pine from Nekoosa's own nursery - a total of 139,500 trees. Some of these will be harvested during the growing cycle to give the remaining trees more room to grow, more sunlight and nutrients. For comparison look at the untreated area to the left and right of the platform.

When the final stand harvest is conducted, around the year 2020, this site will have produced approximately 50 cords of fine raw material per acre - about 35 more cords per acre than was produced by the less intensively managed natural forest - enough raw material to provide 1,550,000 reams of fine writing and printing paper.

Your forest industry using intensive management provides all of us with a habitat for wildlife and a place for recreation.

TREES ARE AMERICA'S RENEWABLE RESOURCE.

Both of these forest industry waysides have the same purpose. They explain forest management practices, often a public relations problem. Which message do you feel is most successfully communicated?

The simple understatement of the Rayonier sign promises that the forest will be renewed.

Industrial forest site, Olympic Peninsula, Washington

Michael Gross

How to Plan Signs and Wayside Exhibits

Develop an intimate understanding of the site. Special feelings you have will emerge in your interpretation.

Immerse yourself in the site. Are there special sensations or animal activities at a particular time of day or season? Can signs make visitors aware of them?

Investigate the facts. What stories are told about this place? Read. Talk to people who know.

Understand the visitor. Use surveys. Why do they come to this place? Take the perspective of as many of your visitors as possible. How does this place look from the level of a child or a person in a wheelchair?

Listen to visitors. Learn their questions, feelings, impressions. What do they want to know?

Define your purpose. Write your specific objectives in simple sentences. Your objectives may be to convey a fact, a feeling, or stimulate an action.

Create a sign that achieves your objectives in the most simple and elegant way.

The "Bizarro" cartoon by Dan Piraro is reprinted by permission of Chronicle Fatures, San Francisco, CA.

Case Studies in Sign and Wayside Planning

Case Study 1 - Mount Saint Helens National Volcanic Monument

Mount Saint Helens National Volcanic Monument, Washington

Dahn Design

Courtesy, USDA Forest Service

The eruption of Mount Saint Helens on May 18, 1980 provided an unparalleled opportunity to answer the questions of a public hungry for information. The story of catastrophic geologic forces, human tragedy, and the tenacity of life are the elements of a compelling story.

The interpretive staff at the newly created Mount Saint Helens National Volcanic Monument had to act quickly to provide accurate, yet concise information to visitors on the site. Wayside exhibits were an important part of a comprehensive interpretive plan.

A team was formed which included a supervisory interpreter, writers, artists, graphic designers, landscape architects, and representatives from the supervisor's office.

The writing team took a holistic approach. It is a model that you may wish to follow. You will be rewarded with signs that answer imporant visitor questions in a consistent and thematic way.

Steps in Planning the Mount Saint Helens Way

- **Develop a Common Vision**
  Take the team to the sites interpreted. Try to look at the site as though you are a first-time visitor. This visit can give you insight into the questions and feelings that visitors might have. Everyone's thoughts and emotions should be recorded. Gain insight by observing visitors and interviewing them.

- **Brainstorm**
  While the impressions are fresh and still developing, brainstorm the possibilities as a team. It is important to maintain a free-wheeling, non-judgmental atmosphere. Even the wildest ideas should be recorded. Identify a brainstorming facilitator who records ideas on an easel for all to see.
  The core purposes for each sign is explored. "The visitor should feel frailty of life and our own lack of power and control." "The visitor should know the scale of destruction in those first few moments of the blast."

- **Research and Inventory**
  Research is necessary to develop your stories and insure accuracy. The team should collect reports and photographs that document the facts. Identify and interview people who have special knowledge about the site. These may be experts or locals. Record these interviews in a notebook. Listen carefully for metaphors, analogies, and phrases that your resource specialists use. These may give a breath of life to otherwise cold abstractions.

- **Set Final Themes and Objectives**
  This step verifies that the team is focusing on the same big ideas. Identify specific themes that will be developed in your interpretive signs. Write objectives for each sign. Objectives should reflect the emotions and knowledge you wish to convey or the actions you wish your visitors to take. It considers the visitor, the stories of the site, the agency, and effective methods of communication.

- **Craft the Message**
  Your message is a wedding of words and visuals. Each affects and amplifies the other. Graphic artists and writers must work together.
  The Mount Saint Helens team wrote a series of drafts, each a refinement of the preceding, until the team agreed that both art and text told the story in a concise and stimulating way.

- **Construct a Mock-Up**
  Construct an inexpensive mock-up for visitors to test. From cosmetics to airplanes, products are tested before they go into production. A field test of your sign can tell you if you are connecting with the visitor.
  Observe visitors as they interact with your sign. Do they read the entire message? Talk to them. Do they still have questions that aren't being answered? Have they been moved or provoked? Do they have any suggestions?
  Use their suggestions to adjust your message. Once a sign is set in fiberglass, metal, or wood, changes are unlikely.

Case Study 2 - San Diego Wild Animal Park

Zoos also rely on interpretive signs to communicate with visitors. It is rare, if not impossible, to interpret the dynamic behavior of animals with signs in the wild. In controlled settings, signs placed at observation points can answer common and predictable questions.

San Diego Wild Animal Park consistently achieves high quality in their interpretive signs. They have created a graphics manual so that all staff members work from a common philosophy. Parts of this manual are reproduced on page 51.

Photos by Michael Gross

Visitor involvement is a primary objective for San Diego Wild Animal Park.

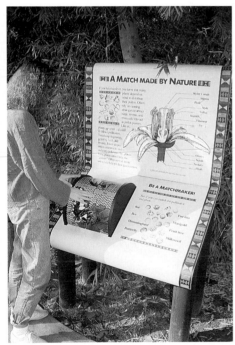

A Match Made by Nature challenges the visitor to spin the wheels and match pollinators with their flower.

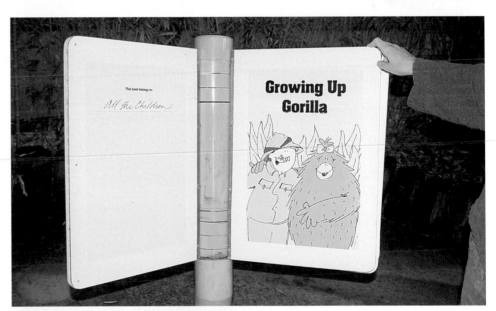

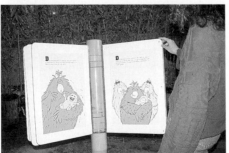

Wild Animal Park signs engage children and adults. The storybook format of *Growing Up Gorilla* is particularly appropriate for younger children.

The Wild Animal Park is renowned for its breeding program of endangered species. Several panels tell that story.

Engaging titles, brief messages, and dramatic graphics ensure a high fraction of selection for Wild Animal Park panels.

Signs are placed at strategic viewing points.

Longer messages are placed along the tramway waiting line.

Excerpts from Wild Animal Park Manual

This graphics manual has helped the San Diego Wild Animal Park achieve uniformity in content and graphics. Quality is achieved by employing professional writers and artists. Contracted writers and artists use the manual to learn the park philosophy, sign parameters, and production standards.

Educational signs are silent yet eloquent hosts to guests.

The graphics content will convey information in ways that...inspire our guests...

The Wild Animal Park is perhaps the only zoo that was created for animals, not for people...

These are characteristics of visitors to the San Diego Wild Animal Park:...:

The fictitious person behind our graphics voice: ...is suscinct. Is visionary about wildlife...

Content Guidelines for Graphics

Education Department
San Diego Wild Animal Park

Table of Contents

Steps to Include in Content Development

1. **Identify visitors' questions/comments about the topic.**
   - listen/eavesdrop at the exhibit
   - ask visitors what they would like to know
   - put a tape recorder or comment board at the exhibit
   - ask keepers and other employees what visitors inquire about
   - ask tour guides what visitors ask them
   - brainstorm questions with the exhibit team

2. **Use questions and directions to psychologically project visitors into the exhibit.**
   - e.g., compare your hand to a gorilla's (handprint)
   - e.g., which is the female?

3. **Plan all graphics together.**
   - directional
   - interpretive
   - donor
   - plant

4. **Include different levels/types of information.**
   - illustrations
   - peep holes
   - touchables
   - details
   - stories
   - video
   - sounds
   - photographs
   - appropriate humor

5. **Select topics and develop text that is imagable.**

6. **Offer different kinds of physical experiences.**
   - look closely
   - peek
   - reach
   - push
   - lift
   - feel
   - listen
   - find
   - turn
   - wonder
   - smell
   - touch

7. **Get visitors to read to each other.**
   - use large type
   - place graphic at eye level
   - use short sentences and paragraphs
   - ask questions
   - use catchy phrases
   - use humor

Make the text readable.
   - refer to things the visitor can see
   - use words that direct the visitor to observe and/or participate
   - answer commonly-asked questions
   - offer games and humor
   - give feedback
   - organize--chronological order; cause and effect; problem, analysis, solution; order of importance; part to whole or whole to part
   - tell a story
   - correct misconceptions
   - use subheads--sentences that summarize
   - build in rhythm and internal rhyme
   - use parallelism
   - repeat
   - compare and contrast

Introduction

Educational signs are silent yet eloquent hosts to guests who visit the San Diego Wild Animal Park. When visitors approach an enclosure, enter an aviary, or wonder about a plant or animal, our graphics can stimulate ideas, answer questions, and help visitors understand our message.

Because the function of our graphics program is so important, we have developed these content guidelines. They help us create graphic content in a consistent manner, from a common point of view, and with intentional messages.

The uses of this document are primarily:
- *training for new employees and consultants*
- *platform for consistency for writers and editors*

Communicating Rules With Signs

To the recreation-area manager, rules are purposeful, valuable, and necessary for the proper maintenance of the environment and for the protection of people. Recreationists, however, do not always recognize the worth of rules, because they do not agree with them, do not understand them, or simply do not know about them. Better methods are needed to tell what the rules are. (Ross and Mueller, *Communicating Rules in Recreation Areas)*

Recommendations for Communicating Rules

- Place rules where visitors are sure to see them. Entrances, bulletin boards, and especially restrooms, give visitors time to read them.

- Be provocative. Even when placed properly, signs will not be read unless they command attention through colors, graphics, and vivid, concise wording.

- State rules in a positive tone. A hostile or dogmatic tone will create resentment and noncompliance. Friendly graphics can support a positive tone.

- Give the reader reasons for the rules.

Information boards at trailheads are commonly used to communicate rules. They must command attention and appeal for compliance.

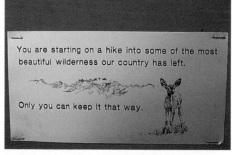

Olympic National Park, Washington

Uinta National Forest, Utah

Rocky Mountain National Park, Colorado
Proper placement of signs can reduce destructive behavior.

Clearwater National Forest, Idaho

Photos by Michael Gross

Rocky Mountain National Park, Colorado

State rules in simple direct language. People have more respect for rules if they know the reasons for them.

Photos by Michael Gross

Corkscrew Swamp Audubon Sanctuary, Florida

Aransas National Wildlife Refuge, Texas

LBJ Ranch, Texas

San Diego Wild Animal Park, California

Rules can be stated in a positive, light-hearted way.

Blue Springs State Park, Florida

Key Deer National Wildlife Refuge, Florida
Photos courtesy of Wilderness Graphics

San Diego Wild Animal Park, California

Aransas National Wildlife Refuge, Texas

Mt. Hood National Forest, Oregon

Everglades National Park, Florida

Photos by Michael Gross

Orienting with Signs

People need signs to find their way. Signs stay on the job even when the visitor center is closed. Prominent features that can be seen should be clearly identified on orientation maps. A "You are here" indicates the visitor's location.

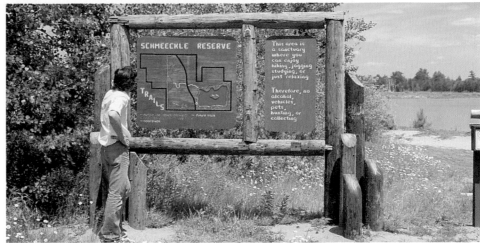

Schmeeckle Reserve

Schmeeckle Reserve

This unobtrusive sign answers a common question.

Mosquito Hill Nature Center, Wisconsin — Jim Anderson

Be as direct as possible. This relief carving is rendered to scale and oriented to the landscape.

Brookfield Zoo, Chicago — Donna Zimmerman

Simple graphics are more efficient than words for orientation.

Scenic vistas are natural locations for visitor orientation.
Photo by Michael Gross
Rocky Mountain National Park

Information Boards

Mount Saint Helens National Volcanic Monument, Washington

Jim Gale, USDA Forest Service

Bulletin boards are among the most commonly used and neglected forms of visitor communication. The Mount Saint Helens interpreters approached bulletin boards from a new perspective. They renamed them "information boards."

Tips for Information Boards

- Organize the board for quick scanning. Use headings, subtitles and symbols. Avoid cluttering the panel.

- Colors and shapes should be interesting and pleasing.

- Use vivid, active language in titles.

- Information should be site-specific and of immediate use to the visitor.

- Information boards should be kept current. Vigorously prune outdated material and replace with current and seasonal events.

5
Sign Fabrication

Photo series on crafting wood signs, courtesy Handcrafted Cedar Sign Shop, Schmeeckle Reserve, University of Wisconsin, Stevens Point

When asked, visitors to natural areas say they prefer to see few, if any, signs. They are seeking an experience in a pristine environment. Signs are considered an intrusion.

Signs must strike a balance between meeting a visitor's need for information and keeping the site natural. Rustic, routed wood is often the best choice for natural areas. Micro-image metal may be better suited to historical or cultural sites. A zoo may require the vivid colors of porcelain enamel.

Technical skill alone is not enough to create good signs. There must be harmony between materials, design, and the site. This requires insight and a well-developed sense of aesthetics. Sign creation should not be delegated to specialists. Even the most skilled carpenter cannot be expected to create an effective wood sign. Someone with a sensitivity to all aspects of the project should work with the technicians.

The technologies and tools for fabricating signs are virtually unlim-ited. Many companies specialize in one or more aspects of sign fabrication. Some specialists' work has been used to illustrate this book. (See Resources for firms that might help you with your project.)

If you choose to create your signs, many options are available to you. Few commercial companies work extensively in wood. With training and a few simple tools, unique and artistic three-dimensional signs are possible.

Crafting Wood Signs

Wood signs blend in with natural environments, trees, foliage, shrubbery, stone, or water. Beautiful landscapes and architecture are least disturbed by unobtrusive, wood signs. As wood signs age, they impart an impression of permanence.

Patrick Spielman
from *Making Wood Signs*

Be resourceful! Creativity, patience, and a few simple tools can create professional-appearing signs. The only limitation to your creativity is the need for uniformity in your sign system. Sign supports, panels, and faces should be similar in color, typeface, and material.

Denali National Park and Preserve, Alaska   Donna Zimmerman
This wood sign reflects the wild qualities of the park.

Denali National Park and Preserve, Alaska
The bear was cut, carved and glued to the sign face.

Ron Zimmerman
Alaska signs must absorb gunshot. Wood is the natural choice.

Tools and Materials

At a minimum, you will need a router, bits, and clamps. Materials may be as basic as wood, exterior glue, and paint.

Basic tools.

Basic materials.

Gluing and Clamping

Sign panels should be clamped and glued with an exterior grade glue. The larger the surface area of the sign, the thicker the wood. On very large panels, threaded rods assure durability.

Image Transfer

Every routed sign begins with a pattern, text, and graphics that are transferred to a wooden sign face.

Text can be generated by laser printers or lettering machines. Images can be copies from photographs or original art.

Refer to Chapter Two for fundamentals of lettering and graphic design.

Transfer the pattern with an overhead projector to produce the desired size. A photocopier is used to make the transparency.

As an alternative, a photocopier can reduce or enlarge the copy and then transferred to the sign face with carbon paper.

Some sign makers use templates and stencils for lettering. However, these devices often produce a sterile, institutional look.

Routing and Carving

When routing signs, choose a sharp, appropriate bit and maintain control with a shallow cut pulling the router toward you. A good light source is essential to accurately follow lines. Ear and eye protection are a must.

A hand-carved effect is achieved by routing around a drawing and then chiseling the edges.

Nancy Cripe

This sign was created by a university student in her first attempt.

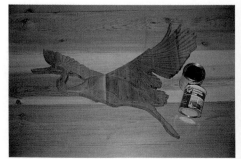

Dramatic relief can be obtained by carving a cut-out and gluing it onto a sign face.

"Dremel tools" and other rotary cutters speed up sculpting and allow inexperienced carvers to do detailed work.

Fort Wayne Children's Zoo, Indiana   Randy Korb

Combinations of layering and carving create special effects.

Finishing

High quality sign paints pay for themselves in lower maintenance. Water sealers and other finishes protect sign faces, but may not be desirable for rustic signs.

Sandblasted Signs

Sandblasted signs accentuate wood grain and create a three dimensional effect. It is a simple process of blasting sand on the panel through a high pressure air system. A commercial masking material is cut to create a stencil and prevents abrasion of the wood under it. Sandblasted signs are even easier to make than carved signs.

Callaway Gardens, Georgia

Michael Gross

Key Deer National Wildlife Refuge, Florida
Photo courtesy of Wilderness Graphics

Photos below courtesy of 3-M Corporation

A stencil is cut in Scotch™ Brand Letter Perfect material.

The resilient rubber backing shields the desired relief areas as they are sandblasted.

The stencil produces a clean and sharp-edged relief.

Silkscreen Imaging

Photos and text courtesy of Marvin Cook, **Wilderness Graphics, Inc.**, Post Office Box 1635, Tallahassee, Florida 32302

Just as each sign material has individual characteristics, technical aspects of production for sign mediums vary. Etched metal and some porcelain enameled sign faces are produced through photochemical processes. Silkscreening is used on aluminum, plexiglass, or plywood and paper for fiberglass embedment.

These technical production factors provide a wide range of colors, graphic illustrations, photographic images, and typography. It is important to match sign design with the limitations of the sign medium. Colors suitable for printed publications may not be suitable for outdoor exhibits.

The following photos illustrate a step-by-step fabrication process for development of an outdoor exhibit panel with silkscreen imaging.

Design and Layout

From a design concept and written copy, the designer produces a scale layout that includes color and graphics. A typestyle is selected and copy is sized and edited to fit the layout.

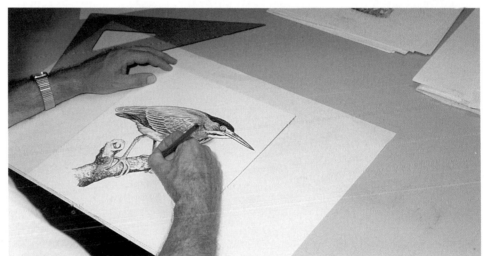

Graphic illustrations are produced in a style suitable for screen printing.

The copy is typeset in the size and style specified by the designer.

The typeset galleys are proofed for typographical errors.

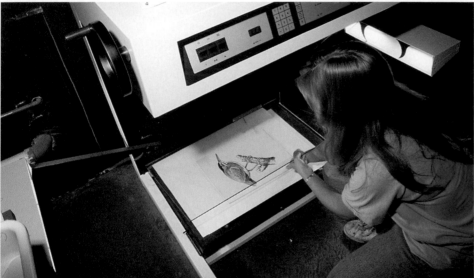

The illustrations and typeset copy are photographed with a graphic arts camera to produce film positives.

Film positives are positioned in place according to the design in a procedure called stripping. This principal image is used to register overlays for each additional color.

Creating Silkscreen Stencils

The overlays may be additional graphics or color areas made from a film, called rubylith, which blocks out light.

Fabric, stretched over frames, is used to carry photographically produced stencils. Various meshes of fabric are used according to desired detail of image.

Each overprinting color requires a separate silkscreen stencil.

The silkscreens are imaged by exposing photo-sensitized stencil or fabric coating to a strong source of UV light. The image is developed and applied to the stretched fabric.

Stencil films are hand cut for background colors. Screens are then checked and prepared for printing.

The substrate is sized and registered for printing.

Silkscreen Printing

Each color is printed by pulling a squeegee across the screen with smooth, even pressure to force ink through openings in the stencil.

Multiple prints should be made during silkscreen printing. It is a good idea to make duplicate substrate signs at this time. Printing of multiple carrier sheets for fiberglass embedment is a standard practice.

Installation

A sign structure is often fabricated concurrently with signs. Aluminum or wood frames and support structures are the most frequently used materials. It is important to coordinate the sign with the framing so there are adequate margins on the sign face and adequate expansion areas in the frames. Most signs will require some support structure and backing.

The finished sign is installed in a support structure.

The sign and structures are installed. Lee Westenburg

Sign Mounting Options

Sign mounting must serve three needs:

• The message must be accessible to all readers.

• The sign must be resistant to vandals and the elements.

• The sign must be unobtrusive to the site.

Olympic National Park, WA   Michael Gross

Sign faces set at an angle are unobtrusive at a distance, but readable when approached. Proper height and angles allow easy reading for tall adults, children, or people in wheelchairs. Sign placement should prevent reflection from sunlight.

Padre Island National Seashore, TX   Michael Gross

A complex series of signs and wayside exhibits can be organized and clustered. Walk-through panels and overhanging roofs invite visitors.

Glacier National Park, Montana   Michael Gross

Larger sign panels require multiple supports. Poured concrete or crossmembers buried in the ground discourage vandalism. Panels can also be attractively mounted in rock walls or railings. Examples are seen in other chapters.

This three panel kiosk, designed by the Fish & Wildlife Service National Sign Center, is silkscreened onto 3/4" high density plywood. The panels withstand submersion during spring flooding. Panels are mounted individually which allows for easy removal for painting or repairing. They are mounted with "theft-proof" vandal-resistant screws. This complex message is understandable because each idea is isolated on its own panel. Seasonal exhibits can be placed on removable panels.

Upper Mississippi River National Wildlife and Fish Refuge

Henry A. Schneider

Unita National Forest, Utah

This trail uses metal and fiberglass signs mounted on wood supports and wood panel backing. The unity of design, from entrance sign to trail panels, shows sensitivity to the landscape.

Photos courtesy of Jim Peters, Interpretive Graphics, Signs and Systems

Accessibility Guidelines for Wayside Exhibits

These National Park Service guidelines were developed by Harpers Ferry Center, Division of Wayside Exhibits. Wayside exhibits should be accessible to all visitors.

Guidelines Affecting Mobility-Impaired Visitors
- Wayside exhibits will be installed at accessible locations wherever possible.
- Wayside exhibit panels will be installed at heights and angles favorable for viewing by most visitors, including those in wheelchairs. For standard NPS low-profile units, the recommended height is 30-34" from the bottom of the exhibit panel to finished grade; for vertical exhibits and bulletin boards the height is 24-28", depending on panel size.
- Trailhead exhibits will include an accessibility advisory.
- Wayside exhibits will have level, hard-surfaced exhibit pads.
- Exhibit sites will offer clean, unrestricted views of park features described in exhibits.

Guidelines Affecting Visually-Impaired Visitors
- Exhibit type will be as legible and readable as possible.
- Panel colors will be selected to reduce eye strain and glare, and to provide excellent readability under field conditions. White should not be used for a background color.
- Selected wayside exhibits may incorporate audiostations or tactile elements such as models, texture blocks, and relief maps.
- For all major features interpreted by graphic wayside exhibits, the park should offer non-visual interpretation covering the same subject matter. Examples include cassette tape tours, radio messages, and ranger talks.
- Use the table on page 11 for letter sizes for the visually impaired.

Guidelines Affecting Hearing-Impaired Visitors
- Wayside exhibit panels will communicate visually, and will rely heavily on graphics to interpret park resources.
- Essential information included in audiostation messages will be duplicated in written form, either as part of the exhibit text, or in a publication.

Guidelines Affecting Learning-Impaired Visitors
- Topics for wayside exhibits will be specific and of general interest. Unnecessary complexity will be avoided.
- Wherever possible, easy-to-understand graphics will be used to convey ideas, rather than text alone.
- Unfamiliar expressions, technical terms, and jargon will be avoided. Pronunciation aids and definitions will be provided where needed.
- Text will be concise and free of long paragraphs and wordy language.

6
Trails - Corridors to Adventure

Two roads diverged in a yellow wood,
And sorry I could not travel both
And be one traveler, long I stood
And looked down one as far as I could
To where it bent in the undergrowth.

Robert Frost
from *The Road Not Taken*

Denali National Park, Alaska   Donna Zimmerman

"There are some who find a trailhead, or a path through the woods which curves invitingly out of sight, simply irresistible. Thoreau was such a person and before him Wordsworth. And today it's me and probably you. It is a romantic idea, surely, a reaction to the organized spaces of an industrial age, with all its square corners and square lives and intentionality. Sometimes we need just to set out, afoot or a-bike, to go where a path takes us...But when a path and a natural scene are joined, the congruence can work powerfully on our imagination. Striding across a meadow, picking one's way along a ridge, or meandering down the banks of a stream makes even ordinary landscapes somehow wonderful."

Charles E. Little
from **Greenways for America**

Designing Trails that Involve People

Trails fill fundamental needs within us. When asked, people say they take trails in search of:

- solitude
- beauty
- new experiences
- meaning/connectedness
- escape from daily stresses or boredom
- self-renewal
- a private place
- peace
- inspiration
- novelty
- comradeship
- romance
- challenge
- memories

Rocky Mountain National Park, Colorado   Michael Gross

Perrot State Park, Wisconsin   Donna Zimmerman

Blue Springs State Park, Florida   Michael Gross

British Columbia   Lloyd Rushton

Mount Washburn Trail, Yellowstone National Park
Photo by Beverly Gross

San Diego Wild Animal Park   Michael Gross

Olympic National Park, Washington   Michael Gross

A well-designed trail offers the possibility of fulfilling these needs. But even a well-planned trail is serendipitous and subject to the whims of nature.

A trail has many moods depending on time of day, weather, or season. A trail in May, alive with migrating warblers, in June is swarming with mosquitoes. Good trail design allows for dynamic possibilities.

Sequence in Schmeeckle Reserve, Wisconsin

Ingredients for Visitor Involvement

Trail design is the process of exposing the mystery, variety, and beauty that a site has to offer. Nearly everything that engages a visitor along a trail can be classified into one or more of these three categories.

Designing for Mystery

Mystery is any feature of a trail that arouses curiosity and provokes the visitor to explore. An observer should be induced to move around the bend or over the crest of a hill to see what lies beyond. Mystery can be:

Enticing trail names.

Stories or artifacts of past events that occurred here.

A trail curving around a bend out of view.

The fragrance of a milkweed blossom.

The lure of a cool, dark canyon.

A vista partially screened by vegetation.

A tantalizing view of a peak that looms in the distance.

Light filtering through a canopy opening.

Sunny openings in the heart of a dense forest that invite entry and exploration.

Distant sound of rushing water.

Lane Cove Greenway, Sydney, Australia — Donna Zimmerman
Overhanging sandstone frames a view of eucalyptus trees on this urban trail.

Schmeeckle Reserve, Wisconsin — Michael Gross
Vegetation can be pruned or removed to frame vistas.

Mount Rushmore National Monument, South Dakota   Michael Gross

Tunnels on the Iron Mountain Road in the Black Hills are designed to frame the faces on Mount Rushmore.

Aransas National Wildlife Refuge, TX, Michael Gross

A provocative trail name, direct invitation, and oyster shell shape lure the visitor onto this trail.

Porcupine Mountain Wilderness, Michigan   Ron Zimmerman

Big trees, a trail curving out of view, and the rush of rapids draw visitors onward. The Manabezho Falls on the Presque Isle River in Michigan's Upper Peninsula are a popular destination. Elaborate staircases promise a rewarding view of the falls.

Designing for Variety

Variety is any feature of a trail that provides contrast, diversity and change. We rebel against monotony. A trail through a plantation of even aged trees soon becomes boring. We enjoy the contrast of big and little trees, mixed undergrowth, forest openings, and rock outcroppings. A word of caution, however; too much variety can be chaotic and create a sense of disorder. Sometimes monotony can be induced in order to enhance or intensify a spectacular view farther along the trail.

Variety can take the form of:

Colors of bark, leaves, flowers, and fruit.

Textures and plant forms.

An area exposed to wind contrasted to one that is sheltered.

A shaded trail that opens on (or into) a sunny meadow.

The perspective of a tower or elevated walkway.

The smell of a sun-soaked pine forest or a prairie pothole.

Contrasting landforms and landscape features.

Changing habitats such as dry forest to swamps to a sandy beach.

British Columbia   Lloyd Rushton

The striking contrast of autumn foliage in a sunny opening is the focal point in this view from a shaded boardwalk.

Point Reyes National Seashore, California   Donna Zimmerman

People naturally seek the highest point possible for a view of a landscape. A panoramic view of the Pacific Coast and the possibility of spotting whales make this vista worth the effort.

Route trails to feature the diversity of the site. Big trees inspire awe. Cathedral-like forests give a sense of shelter and are a tangible link to our primeval past.

Light filtered through a canopy dances from shrubs and ferns. The forest offers a calendar of color in ephemeral flowers, bright fruit, and autumn leaves. Each layer of the forest harbors wildlife to observe.

Redwood National Park, California   Donna Zimmerman

Fraser Island, Queensland, Australia   Donna Zimmerman

Designing for Beauty

Beauty may be described as grace, elegance, or harmony. Everyone recognizes beauty, but nobody can define it.

Most would agree that mystery and variety are attributes of beauty. There is mystery in a river meandering gracefully out of sight. There is very little in one that has been straightened into a channel. Variety provides excitement, but it must be balanced with our need for order. It is the tension between the stimulation of variety and the tranquility of order that gives us pleasure.

Beauty has been defined as the degree that objects and features fit with their surroundings. "Fitness" can be reflected in the dominance of natural elements (colors, forms, texture) and natural processes, and the subordination of human influences.

Human activities frequently disrupt order. An unscreened clear-cut, a dam on a fast flowing river, the constant hum of a distant highway, a powerline cutting across the landscape, or a brightly colored sign lack harmony and order. A pleasing trail must screen objectionable aspects.

Braulio Carillio National Park, Costa Rica   Donna Zimmerman

A panoramic view offers tranquility. The convergence of land, water, and sky creates a sense of order.

Aerial photo, Schmeeckle Reserve, Wisconsin   Dennis Chapman

The harmony of nature is broken by traffic, wires, and straight lines. Vegetation can buffer objectionable sights and sounds.

Porcupine Mountains State Park, Michigan   Ron Zimmerman

This steel bridge achieves beauty through the repetition of line and harmony of color.

Olympic National Park, Washington   Michael Gross

This moss-encrusted wooden bridge in the rain forest fits the landscape. A view to a sunny opening adds variety and interest to the scene.

The straight line of a man-made dike is monotonous and uninviting. Diverse topography and a curving trail invite walkers to explore.

Mead Wildlife Area, Wisconsin   Ron Zimmerman   Perrot State Park, Wisconsin   Donna Zimmerman

Designing for Mystery, Variety, Beauty

Each trail should provide a unique and refreshing adventure. Trail planning is much more than putting a path through the woods. It is a holistic endeavor that includes an understanding of the needs of people and the potential of the site.

- Route trails past the largest trees.

- Manage vegetation for diversity in texture, patterns, and density.

- Introduce or maintain colorful trees, shrubs, and ground covers.

- Plan vistas that allow directed views like lakes, peaks, valleys, and cliffs.

- Create views into forests and other vegetation (selectively cut understory, prune lower branches, thin stands, and create openings). Don't overdo this, however. Be sensitive to the natural form of vegetation and ecological integrity.

- Create forest openings that invite entry.

- Route the trail over running water and under large trees.

- Use structures to provide unique views and vistas.

- Use curves to draw people down trails.

- Screen objectionable views, sounds, or artificial structures.

- Position "views" on trails and boardwalks so the sun is on the visitor's back. This illuminates birds and other subjects for easy viewing.

7

Trail Construction and Maintenance

A well-made and well-maintained trail must be in harmony with the landscape and be inviting and safe to users. Choices in materials and maintenance procedures are determined by the numbers of users and their activities.

Trails can be classified into three broad functions: recreation, interpretation, and education. Some trails may be used for all three. Some uses are incompatible.

Schmeeckle Reserve, Stevens Point, Wisconsin   Ron Zimmerman

Categories of Use	Recreation	Interpretation	Education
Activity Examples	Motoring (scenic byway) Horse-back riding (equestrian) Off-road (ORV) motoring Boating and canoeing Bicycling Hiking Fitness and jogging	Orientation to an area Self-guided learning about natural history of the area Self-guided learning about cultural history of the area Interpreter-guided learning about an area (trams and on foot)	Study at designated trail stations Use of trail as an outdoor classroom Guided exploration involving sensory, conceptual, or factual information
Visitor Mode	Leisure Time Activities	Leisure Time Learning	Formal Learning

Protecting the Trail Environment

Not every site should be invaded by trails. But, if a decision has been thoughtfully made, the next step is to lay out the trail with sensitivity and understanding of the site.

Keep in mind the purpose of the trail. Avoid overconstruction. Most visitors to natural areas value a primitive appearance. A trail should never appear as an intrusion. It should follow the contours of the landscape and be surfaced with materials that blend with the site.

Erosion Control

Trail building starts by getting on your hands and knees. Look at your soil material. Find out what it is composed of and what it does in the rain. Find out where the water comes from before it gets to your trail and where it goes when it leaves. Your prime considereation is slowing and directing the water runoff from your trail surface.

Mark Edwards
Trails Coordinator, Iowa
Department of Natural Resources

Constructing Trails on Slopes

A 0-5 percent (5 percent = 5 foot rise in 100 foot distance) grade is the most comfortable for walking. Inclines of more than 10 percent should be limited to short distances. Slopes over 7-10 percent will need steps, landings, and waterbars to stop erosion. As you approach 50 percent you have passed the point of being able to control erosion.

Left: An improperly surfaced trail retains water. Trail "braiding" results when walkers avoid these wet areas.

Right: Trails on slopes can channel water and create gullies. These conditions must be corrected before severe damage results.

Protecting Wet and Fragile Areas

Some areas are best left inaccessible. Protect them from visitors by distance or visual screening.

Schmeeckle Reserve, Wisconsin

If the trail traverses fragile areas, such as ephemeral groundcovers or wetlands, line the trail with split rails or ropes. Elevated boardwalks also allow observation without entry.

Battle Creek Cypress Swamp Sanctuary, Maryland · Dwight Williams

Central Wisconsin Environmental Station · Michael Gross

Destructive Invaders

Trails open a site to more than human users. Some are destructive. Raccoons, cowbirds, skunks, and other predators gain access on trails and roads. They can displace many native species. Consider the consequences a trail can have on fragile habitats.

Cutting of existing vegetation invites weedy invaders. Introducing sunlight where shade existed does the same. Revegetate with sun-loving native vegetation if this is a problem.

Trails may become travel corridors for deer and other wildlife. By creating new entrances and exits, they may expand your trail system in unplanned ways.

Yellowstone National Park · Michael Gross

Visitor Safety

Visitors seek the security of an identified trail. A trailhead, a sign, or map are an invitation to explore an area. Safety is not an amenity; it is a necessity and a legal obligation.

A well designed trail should not become an "attractive nuisance." Dangerous cliffs, avalanche fields, high wind corridors, lightning prone ridges, or places prone to snowdrifting, bogging or iciness should be avoided.

If hazards cannot be avoided, then warning signs and protection must be provided.

Rocky Mountain National Park   Michael Gross

Well informed visitors are capable of making decisions regarding their own well-being. Signs should set expectations and let users know the exact distances, difficulties, and alternatives they will encounter.

Central WI Environmental Station   Michael Gross

An old snag can become lethal in wind. Remove it if it threatens visitors on the trail.

Central Wisconsin Environmental Station   Michael Gross

Exposed roots and rocks can be dangerous to those who have diminished sight or mobility.

Maintenance

Maintenance Priorities

- **Correct unsafe conditions.**
- **Prevent resource and trail damage.**
- **Provide for visitor convenience and comfort.**

Trail Maintenance Documentation

Trail maintenance logs, people counters, and photo-documentation identify changing conditions.

Larry Van Slyke

An electric eye counts hikers on a popular trail in Zion National Park.

TRAIL LOG AND CONDITION/CORRECTION SURVEY
(from NPS Trails Management Handbook)

Park_____ Trail Name and No. _____

Dist._____ Length_____ Page_____ of _____

Maint. Level:_____ Type of Trail:_____

Logged by:_____ | Surveyed by: _____

Date:_____ | Date: _____

Sta.	Feature	Condition/Correction	Equip.

1980

1991

Documentation of trail changes can be accomplished by periodic photos from trail-side bench marks. These soon take on historic and scientific significance.

Trail Configurations

Interpretive Trails

Most visitors begin an interpretive walk at a parking lot or visitor center where they must return. A loop trail accomplishes this.

Loop Trail Advantages

- **Visitors never see the same portion of the trail twice.**
- **A sense of solitude is enhanced since there are fewer encounters with other hikers.**
- **Only one trailhead is needed, reducing cost and maintenance.**

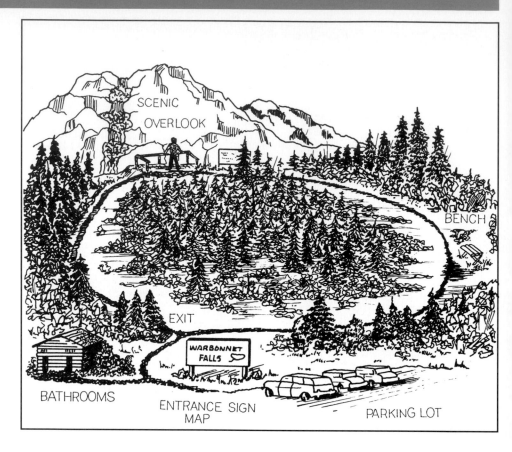

Hiking Trails

Hiking trails may follow a multiple loop configuration. Since travel corridors are frequently linear, loops may not be feasible. Linear or horseshoe configurations may be the only options.

Small Group Teaching Trails

School groups and other educational groups are best accommodated by an orb-web design. Educational groups are typically divided into small teacher-led groups. Class periods require efficient travel to and from learning stations. Equal distances are desirable.

Central Wisconsin Environmental Station

Central Wisconsin Environmental Station

Trail Management Zones

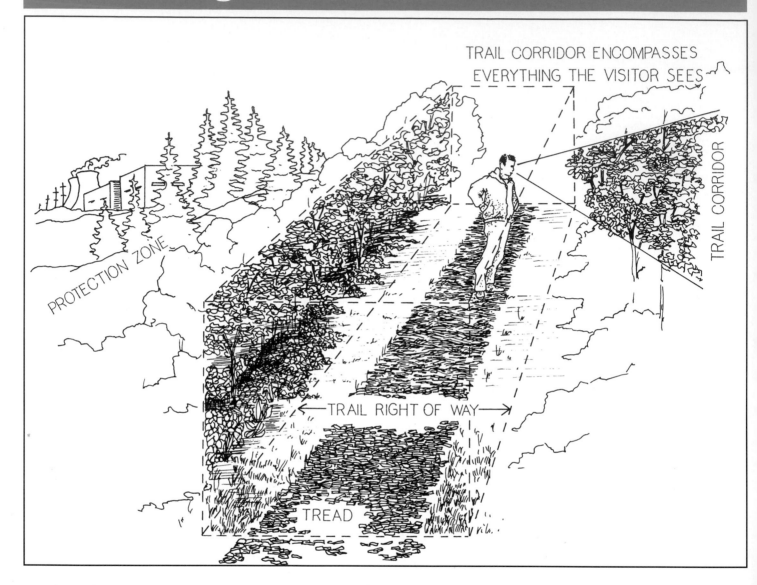

Definitions

Trail treadway or tread: the surface the visitor walks on.

Trail right-of-way: the area around the treadway that is cleared for safety.

Trail corridor: the combination of the treadway, right-of-way, and all the land the visitor sees along the trail and that influences their perception of the trail.

Buffer or protection zone: the land that insulates the hiker from activities adjacent to the trail that might be detrimental to the hiking experience including home development, mining, logging. This zone can also serve to protect fragile areas from visitor damage.

Treadway

Trail surfaces affect the visitor visually, acoustically, and tactilly. When they work, trail surfaces go unnoticed; when they don't, they become the focus of frustration. Mud, unwanted noise, and unstable footing can ruin a walk experience even when the vistas are grand and wildlife is abundant. Trail surfaces are an unglamorous utilitarian feature fundamental to visitor needs - choose them carefully.

Trail surface materials are determined by:
- Amount of visitor use
- Characteristics of the substrate
- Aesthetic compatibility with the site
- Cost

Generally, more traffic demands more resilient surfaces. Main trails, such as those connecting visitor centers to parking lots, might require asphalt or crushed rock. If your site experiences spring melt or high groundwater, a boardwalk could be a necessity. In the other extreme, a short loop trail through a small meadow might only need mowing to accommodate a few visitors. Bird watchers seeking solitude may prefer little more than a pruned game trail that discourages group use.

Surface	Applications	Advantages	Disadvantages	Suggestions
Asphalt (asphalt with sand and epoxy pounded into it provides a rough surface that prevents slipping)	Heavy Use Wheelchair Access	Little maintenance.	High initial cost. Often looks unnatural. Expensive. Subject to cracking. Tacky in hot sun.	Allow vegetation to grow over edges for natural appearance and coat surface with an epoxy/sand mixture (brand name Darwell).
Soil Cement (cement mixed with local parent material like gravel)	Heavy Use Wheelchair Access	More visually appealing than asphalt.	Expensive.	Crown slightly for drainage.
Paving Stones	Heavy Use	Allows water for infiltration. Attractive surface.	Installation labor intensive. Expensive.	Use mechanical vibrator to set stones.
Gravel (limestone/granite)	Heavy Use	Inexpensive. Allows for water infiltration.	Noisy. Not good for wildlife observation trails.	Weeds invade if not applied in deep layer.
Woodchips	Medium Use	Natural appearance. Easy application.	Can become soggy in poorly drained areas. Requires replenishment.	Hardwood chips are most desirable. Avoid material with sharp and angular chunks due to dull chipping machines.
Shredded Bark	Low/Medium Use	Visually appealing/natural, soft surface.	Breaks down quickly. Only available near saw mills.	Effective in dry areas - preferred by runners and joggers.
Grass	Low Seasonal Use	Aesthetically appealing in open areas.	Requires a recovery period.	Use where alternative routes allow recovery.
Natural Surface	Wilderness/Low Use	Minimal maintenance.	Can easily degenerate into fragments and braided trails.	Use markers and maps.

Accessability Considerations

Hard surface allows access for visitors with disabilities. Trails should include a gutter on one side and a kickboard on the other to aid the visually impaired. Wheelchairs require grades of less than one foot rise to every 18 feet. A 5-foot width is needed to allow wheelchairs to pass each other.

Trail Surfaces

Glacier National Park, Montana   Alan Capelle

Schlitz Audubon Center, Milwaukee   Michael Gross

Heavily used trails may actually appear more natural when an appropriate hard surface is chosen. They resist erosion and are accessible to most visitors.

Schmeeckle Reserve crushed granite trail

Schmeeckle Reserve. Woodchips fit a forest environment.

Keeweenaw Peninsula, MI   Donna Zimmerman

Locally quarried stone on a frequently wet trail provides a safe surface.

Monte Verde Preserve, Costa Rica Donna Zimmerman

Schmeeckle Reserve   Dennis Chapman

Grass may be sufficient where traffic is seasonal or light.

Left: Wood blocks are covered with wire mesh to prevent slipping on a perpetually wet trail.

Schmeeckle Reserve   Ron Zimmerman

This simple boardwalk protects a vernal wet woods.

Trail Corridor Management

This right-of-way lacks visual interest.

The undulating pattern of this right-of-way cut adds visual interest.

A more intricate pattern of vegetation adds mystery and variety to a walker's view.

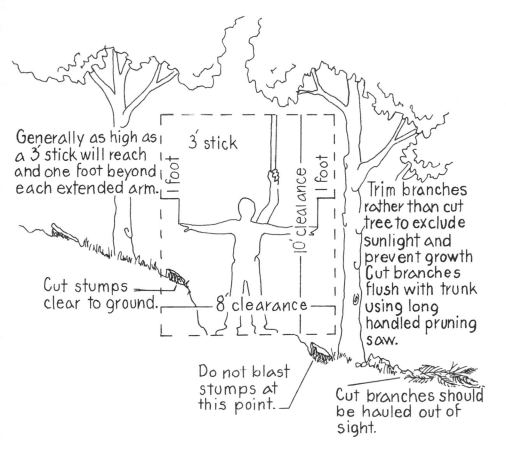

Generally as high as a 3' stick will reach and one foot beyond each extended arm.

3' stick

1 foot

10' clearance

1 foot

Cut stumps clear to ground.

8' clearance

Trim branches rather than cut tree to exclude sunlight and prevent growth. Cut branches flush with trunk using long handled pruning saw.

Do not blast stumps at this point.

Cut branches should be hauled out of sight.

Suggested clearance for interpretive trail. This will accommodate two people walking side by side.

Schmeeckle Reserve

Trails maintained for high use require vehicle access and must be 5-6 feet wide for utility vehicles and 8-10 for trucks.

Trail Structures

Structures can add to the charm and useability of a trail or they can detract from its beauty. Design and construction books are listed in "Resources."

Schmeeckle Reserve

Seating

Well-placed benches invite visitors to pause, reflect, or observe nature. They can be a simple log, split log, or a construction of lumber.

Big Thicket National Preserve, TX   Michael Gross

Glacier National Park, Montana   Michael Gross

Bridges

Water crossings can be as unobtrusive as a culvert or have as much character as a suspension bridge.

Multnomah Falls, Oregon   Michael Gross

Badlands National Park   Ron Zimmerman

North Country National Trail, Hiawatha National Forest, Michigan   Michael Gross

Boardwalks

Boardwalks keep feet dry. When elevated, they give a fresh perspective.

Everglades National Park, Florida   Michael Gross
An elevated boardwalk on Mahogany Trail takes visitors into the treetops.

Trail of the Cedars, Glacier National Park, Montana   Michael Gross
This cedar takes on special significance when incorporated into the boardwalk.

Corkscrew Swamp Audubon Sanctuary, Florida   Michael Gross
A bald cypress swamp is accessible only on this mile-long boardwalk. This internationally renowned trail is a favorite haunt of naturalists and photographers.

Beaver Meadows, Rocky Mountain National Park, Colorado   Michael Gross
Motorists on Trail Ridge Road can get a close view of a beaver pond.

Viewing Blinds

The opportunity to see wildlife is a strong incentive to explore a trail. Blinds provide a close-up look.

Santa Anna National Wildlife Refuge, Texas   Michael Gross

Towers

Towers are popular, but a potential eyesore and liability.

Aransas National Wildlife Refuge, Texas   Michael Gross

The promise of seeing whooping cranes from a tower draws visitors across a saltflat. An interpretive sign, "Which white bird is this?" helps visitors to identify cranes, pelicans, storks, and other white birds. Trees soften the appearance of the structure and help it fit into the site.

Everglades National Park, Florida   Paul Trapp

Wading birds, often concealed by pond vegetation, are more easily seen from this elevated platform. An interpretive panel on the rail helps viewers to identify common birds of Eco Pond.

8

Trail Interpretation

*Recreational development is a job not of building roads into lovely country,
but of building receptivity into the still unlovely human mind.*

Aldo Leopold
A Sand County Almanac

View from trail overlook, Portage Glacier, Alaska

Ron Zimmerman

Civilization has removed people from firsthand experiences. The trail experience can be a sensory, intellectual and emotional immersion. A person on a trail is rediscovering his or her roots and place on the earth. In the process, they are learning about themselves.

Interpretation should assist in this discovery. The challenge to interpreters is to help people find meaning in these experiences. It is a formidable challenge, but the highest purpose of a park is to help people realize their connection to the land.

Since everyone experiences something different on a trail, a personal visit with an interpreter is a good way to help them find meaning. Nothing beats person to person interpretation.

However, since we cannot spend time with every visitor, we must rely on alternatives.

Alternatives for Trail Interpretation

	Mode of Interpretation	Advantages	Disadvantages
Personal, spontaneous modes	**Interpreter-led walk**	Personal interaction is the most effective way to develop themes and stories.	Relatively few contacts. Some group members may not "tune in." Expensive.
	Roving interpreter on trail	Most individualized form of interpretation.	Frequently only information is provided, not insight. Usually limited to brief encounters.
Impersonal and inflexible modes	**Pamphlet or booklet** that introduces the general story of the site	Can be read before or after hiking the trail. A detailed story can be told through graphics and text. There is no impact on the site.	Does not provide specific information about what is being immediately experienced and cannot answer questions the visitor may have.
	Leaflet and marker	The only physical imposition on the site is the numbered post. An effective technique for auto tours.	Reading literature while standing on a trail is unnatural. Leaflet can become litter.
	Trail signs	Available to all visitors. Interprets objects or site directly. Flexibility exists to change individual signs.	They are a physical imposition on the site. Expensive, initially; subject to vandalism. Requires reading by standing visitors.
	Audio trails	A human voice allows first person interpretation to humanize story. It is easier to listen than to read. Often a good choice for cultural interpretation.	Seldom suitable for outdoor sites. Requires sophisticated equipment and professional production to be effective.

Guided Walks and Roving Interpretation

Apostle Islands National Lakeshore   Michael Gross

If staffing permits, this is the best choice for trail interpretation.

"Next to the real thing, people in face to face communication are best, and there are a number of ways that spoken words from living lips can interpret."

Yorke Edwards
from *The Land Speaks: Organizing and Running an Interpretation System*

Techniques for interpreter-led programs are detailed in *Presentation Skills for Interpreters,* another book in the Interpreter's Handbook Series.

General Appreciation Publication

A well-designed and well-written general brochure about a site or trail allows visitors to learn about the site at a convenient time. They are free to experience a site without signs.

If distributed at an entrance station or visitor center, there is no sign, marker, or leaflet boxes to mar the landscape. Publications communicate beyond the confines of the park. They can be read in the living room, car, or campsite.

Techniques for writing and designing publications are detailed in *Creating Environmental Publications,* another handbook in this series.

Leaflet and Marker

Bear Lake Trail, Rocky Mountain National Park

Michael Gross

Rocky Mountain National Park   Michael Gross

Leaflet and marker walking trails are seldom effective. The written word is not the story. The story surrounds the visitor. It is unnatural to read an abstract message as you venture down a real trail full of happenings. Visitor observation has documented that few people read publications on a trail. Although often used, we do not recommend this method for trail interpretation.

Leaflet and marker interpretation can be successfully used for car touring. The Trail Ridge Road Guide in Rocky Mountain National Park is popular with motorists visiting the park. Graphically appealing, it uses active, engaging text to share the story of Trail Ridge Road.

Techniques for Effective Leaflet and Marker Interpretation

- **Have a theme that unifies the story and sounds exciting.**

- **Use provocative titles at each station.**

- **Write concise and exciting inscriptions for each stop.**

- **Limit interpretation to the minimum number of stations needed to tell the story. Visitors soon tire of this medium. (The Trail Ridge Road Guide has 12 stops, an optimal number.)**

- **Incorporate strong graphics and illustrations to help tell the story.**

Trail Signs

"Let's free the hands of the visitors, so their eyes, nose, and ears can be attuned to the actual on-site experiences."
Tanner Pilley
Interpretive Media Specialist
National Park Service

Olympic National Park

Michael Gross

Signs are being used more frequently for trail interpretation. Signs can be constructed in a variety of media, incorporate graphics, and be placed next to the features being interpreted. A word of caution: They still require the visitor to read while standing. Studies verify that few visitors choose to read the message. Signs also impose on the landscape. A significant number of people must use the trail to justify the expense and upkeep of a sign.

If, after careful consideration, you choose to interpret with trail signage, adherence to basic principles can increase effectiveness. Chapters Two through Five provide a detailed treatment of these principles. Additional tips are included in the box on the right.

Techniques for Effective Sign-in-Place Trails

- **Have an inviting trailhead that includes an engaging trail name.**

- **Use an introductory sign to set the theme of the trail and indicate trail length. This sign usually has a longer message. On some trails, this may be the only interpretation needed or desired.**

- **All signs must have a provocative title, graphics, and minimal text.**

- **Many interpretive sign specialists recommend that the majority of interpretive signs be placed early on the trail while the visitor is still fresh and interested. Avoid placing two signs in view of each other.**

- **Place signs at natural stopping points and where people have questions.**

- **Limit signs to maintain visitor interest.**

- **Use panel sizes of 30" x 18" for major trail panels, 7" x 5" for identification panels. Mount at a 35-45 degree angle to the ground. (Recommendations by Tanner Pilley.)**

- **Signs should be placed to avoid ruining pristine areas and scenic views.**

Trail Sign Interpretation

Beaver Meadows Boardwalk, Rocky Mountain National Park, Colorado   Michael Gross

Graphics help visitors to better understand the written message.

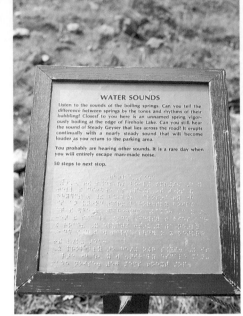

Yellowstone National Park, WY   Michael Gross

Only a small percentage of sight-impaired people can read braille. It is not often used for trail interpretation.

Badlands National Park, South Dakota   Ron Zimmerman

Real fossils, protected by domes, are interpreted on this trail.

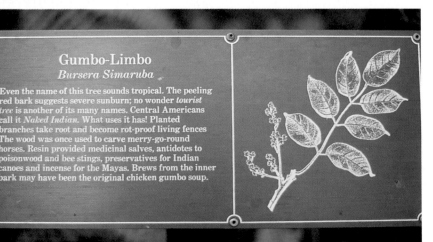

Everglades National Park, Gumbo Limbo Trail, Florida

This inscription uses active language and personalizes the subject.

Michael Gross

Audio Trails

Information and photos courtesy of Chris Tellis, Director of Audio Tours, **Antenna, Inc.**, P.O. Box 176, Sausalito, CA 94966

Voices and sounds can make a site come alive for visitors. New technologies in cassette, FM, infrared, and hidden speaker systems make audio tours an attractive choice for trail interpretation.

An audio tour specialist or experienced AV consultant can help select the most appropriate technology. Generally, headset systems are best used indoors or at historic sites since natural areas provide their own sounds. (Production Tips for Audio Messages can be found on page 35.)

The Alcatraz Cellhouse Audio Tour

Visitors to Alcatraz Island Federal Correctional Facility in San Francisco learn what it was like to live and work on the island. Events at Alcatraz from 1934 to 1963 are recreated on a 43 minute tour using taped narration and a rechargeable, stereo, portable cassette player.

Former correctional officers narrate this award winning tour. Former inmates tell their stories about life on the cellblock. Photos and graphics at each stop give faces to the voices on the tape. Sound effects (the clanging of cell doors, harmonicas at night, the whistles of guards, battle sounds from the 1947 prison riot) bring the story to life.

Taped narration and exhibit panels tell the story of prison life on "Broadway," the main courtyard of the prison.

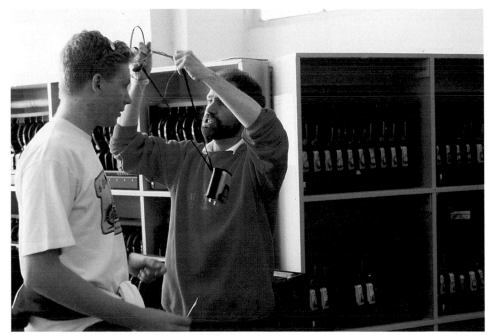

Almost one million visitors annually take the audio tour. Players are stored in recharging units when not in use.

Interpretive Trail Heads

Engaging trail names encourage use of an interpretive trail. Trail heads should set the theme of the trail and provide information about the trail length and special features.

Badlands National Park, SD   Michael Gross

Scotts Bluff National Monument, NE R. Zimmerman

Blue Springs State Park, Florida   Michael Gross

Callaway Gardens, Georgia   Michael Gross

A formal entrance is used at a trail which begins from a parking lot. Motorists need the larger structure to draw them off the road. Interpretation is provided under the canopy.

Callaway Gardens, Georgia   Michael Gross

A small entrance sign and a canopied bulletin board attract visitors who are on foot.

Wasatch National Forest, Utah   Michael Gross

A three-dimensional trail map effectively shows the terrain and distance. A large limber pine is the destination for hikers.

Resources

Measuring Readability

Readability tests can help keep your writing at an easy reading level for your audience. If you use a word processor for writing, you can run a quick readability check with the help of readability testing software.

Flesch Readability Scale

1. Count the number of syllables in a 100 word sample (S).

2. Calculate the average number of words per sentence in the sample (W).

3. Calculate $R = 206.835 - .846S - 1.015W$.

4. Compare value to table:

Score	Reading Ease
90 - 100	very easy
80 - 90	easy
70 - 80	fairly easy
60 - 70	standard
50 - 60	fairly difficult
30 - 50	difficult
0 - 30	very difficult

From *The Art of Readable Writing* by Robert Flesch, 1949.

The Write Formula

1. Count a 100 word sample.

2. Count all one-syllable words except "the," "is," "are," "was," and "were." Count one point for each one-syllable word.

3. Count the number of sentences in the 100-word sample to the nearest period or semicolon and give three points for each sentence.

4. Add together the one-syllable word count and the three points for each sentence to get your grade.

If your piece has less than 100 words, multiply your tally to get the equivalent of 100.

Score	Reading Ease
85 - 100+	Children's Publications
75 - 85	Average American Reader
65 - 75	Above Average American Reader

*A score of 80 is close to ideal.

From *Exhibits for the Small Museum, A Handbook,* by Arminta Neal, 1976.

Books

There are many books to choose from when designing interpretive signs, trails, and wayside exhibits. These are some of the most useful.

Accessibility Standards

Americans with Disabilities Act Handbook
U.S. Employment Opportunity Commision and the U.S. Justice Dept., October, 1992.
For additional information, contact: Public Access Section, Civil Rights Division, U.S. Dept. of Justice, P.O. Box 66118, Washington, DC 20035-6118, (202) 514-0301

Interpretation for Disabled Visitors in the National Park System
David Park, Wendy Ross, W. Ellis
National Park Service, Washington D.C., 1984
U.S. Government Printing Office, Washington, DC 20402

See page 69 of this handbook for The National Park Service Accessibility Guidelines for Wayside Exhibits.

Signs and Wayside Exhibits

Architectural Signing and Graphics
John Follis and Dave Hammer
Whitney Library of Design, Watson-Guptill Publications, New York, NY, 1988
An excellent source for sign makers.

Environmental Interpretation: A Practical Guide for People with Big Ideas and Small Budgets
Sam H. Ham, North American Press, Golden, CO, 1992
An excellent general reference on interpretive media.

The Graphics of Communication
A. Turnbull and R. Baird
4th Ed., New York, NY, 1980
This is an excellent beginners text on graphic design for effective visual communication.

Making Exhibit Labels
Beverly Serrell
American Association for State and Local History
Nashville, TN, 1985

Making Wood Signs
Patrick Spielman
Sterling Publishing Co., Inc., New York, NY, 1981
All aspects of wood sign making are explained.

Noah's Art: Zoo, Aquarium, Aviary and Wildlife Park Graphics
Edited by Wei Yew, 1991, Edmonton, Alberta, Canada, Quon Editions.
Color photo examples from zoos.

Zoo Design: The Reality of Wild Illusions
Kenneth J. Polakowski, School of Natural Resources, University of Michigan, Ann Arbor, MI, 1987.

Trails

Greenways for America
Charles E. Little
Johns Hopkins University Press, Baltimore, MD, 1990
A philosophical treatise on green corridors with many case studies. Beautifully written and illustrated.

Interpretive Trails and Related Facilities Manual
John Veverka and Associates
P.O. Box 26095, Lansing, MI 48909
Designs for trail structures are included in this manual.

NPS Trails Management Handbook
United States Department of the Interior, National Park Service, Denver Service Center, Denver, CO, 1988
U.S. Government Printing No. 1988-576-279/85200

Trail Building and Maintenance 2nd Edition
Robert D. Proudman and Reuben Rajala
Appalachian Mountain Club and National Park Service Trails Program, 1981 (Revised, 1993)
The best source of clearly explained and illustrated trail construction techniques. Available from Appalachian Mountain Club, Box 298, Route 16, Gorham, NH 03581, Phone: (603) 466-2721.

Vandalism

Preventing Cultural Resources Destruction: Taking Action Through Interpretation
Jan S. Ryan, 1992. Free distribution from National Park Service, Div. of Parks Historic Preservation, Western Regional Office, 600 Harrison St., San Francisco, CA 94107-1372, (415) 744-3961

Vandalism Control Management for Parks and Recreation Areas
Monty L. Christiansen
Venture Publishing, Inc., State College, PA, 1982
A complete vandalism control plan for recreation sites.

Working With Designers and Fabricators

Define the project:

- Define your objectives and audiences.
- Write your objectives concisely.
- Determine what you will do yourself and what you will contract:
    - Research and concept development.
    - Development of theme.
    - Development of outlines (one per panel).
    - Development of agency-approved bibliography which provides accurate information.
    - Development of approved common and scientific names.
    - Collect first-person narratives and/or quotes.
    - Write inscriptions.
    - Produce art (drawings or photographs).

Working with a writer:

- Assign a project manager to handle all communications.
- Provide theme and outline.
- Provide agency-approved bibliography.
- Provide approved common and scientific names.
- Provide any first-person narratives or quotations.
- Provide maximum number of words per panel.
- Provide any specific safety, resource protection, preservation information that should be included.
- Confirm in advance who has approval authority at each stage and how many staff members must review and comment.
- Establish mutually agreed-upon time frames for submittal of each stage of work.
- Provide signed approval at each stage.
- Determine in advance how many revisions or rewrites will be covered in the contract.
- Specify in contract whether final is to be hard copy with disc.

Working with an illustrator/designer:

- Assign one project manager to handle all communications.
- Narrow the list of professional designers and fabricators to those that do the type of work you want.
- Further narrow the list by talking to colleagues or references on the quality of their services.
- Confirm that your final selections are interested in bidding on your work.
- Provide detailed information about your project to allow all interested parties to bid on your work. Communicate your decision-making criteria, specifications, timeline, and payment schedule.
- Make a written contract with the service provider. If your project is large or open-ended, be certain your contract is detailed.
- Confirm in advance who has approval authority at each stage and how many staff members must review and comment at each stage.
- Establish mutually agreed-upon time frames for submittal of each stage of work.
- Provide signed approval at each stage.
- Provide clear, detailed description of what is to be illustrated (provide photos, not other illustrations).
- If art is provided, specify in contract whether original art is to be returned to artist.
- Provide information on number of colors and method of fabrication.

Working with a fabricator:

- Have one person designated as the contact person for each party.
- Prior to signing your contract, make certain everyone's roles and responsibilities are clearly defined.
- Make certain colors are clearly specified.
- Establish mutually agreed-upon time frames for production and delivery.
- Clear communication at each step of the process will eliminate wasted work and missed deadlines.

Designers and Fabricators

Audio Tours

Antenna, Inc., Creative Audio Tours, Chris Tellis
P.O. Box 176, Sausalito, CA 94966, (415) 332-4862
Examples page 101.

Tour Mate Systems Limited, Max N. Slivka
449 Adelaide St. W., Toronto, Ontario, Canada M5V 1T1
(416) 594-2376
(Hand held systems)

Planning and Graphic Design

Many of these companies do screen imaging or film preparation and work with fabricators in metal micro-imaging, fiberglass embedment, and porcelain enamel. Some of these companies also provide writing and illustration services.

Command Corporation, Charles E. Ranson, Jr.
116 East Washington St., Charles Town, WV 25414
(304) 725-3212

Companion Press, Jane Freeburg
5266 Hollister, Suite 124, Santa Barbara, CA 93111
(805) 964-5005

Dahn Design, Richard Dahn
1824 NE Ravenna Blvd., Seattle, WA 98105
(206) 525-9325
Examples on pages 15, 20, 47.

Color•Ad Exhibits and Signage
7200 Gary Rd., Manassas, VA 22110
(800) 683-0383

ECOS, Jill Isenhart
2028 17th St., Boulder, CO 80302
(303) 444-3267

Fireside Corporation, Duncan Berry
1715 Smith Tower, Seattle, WA 98104
(206) 623-2428

GS Images, Doug Wright
P.O. Box 1288, Hagerstown, MD 21741-1288
(301) 791-6920

General Graphics, Inc., Bruce Spinnenweber
P.O. Box 1599, Cumberland, MD 21502
(301) 729-1401

The Graphics Group, Florence Bramley, Director
P.O. Box 070216
Staten Island, NY 10307-0002
(718) 317-9800

Great Big Pictures
1444 E. Washington Ave., Madison, WI 53703
240 N. Milwaukee St., Milwaukee, WI 53202
(800) 236-8925

Inside/Outside, Tom Christiansen
2525 Wallingwood Suite 801, Austin, TX 78746
(512) 327-3438

Interpretive Exhibits, Inc., Ed Austin
1865 Beach Ave. N.E., Salem, OR 97303
(503) 371-9411

Interpretive Mgmt. Assoc., Duncan Rollo, Debbie Tewell
263 Aspen Dr., Divide, CO 80814-9692
(719) 687-0160

Interstate Graphics, John V. Norwood
7817 Burden Rd., Rockford, IL 61111
(800) 243-3925, (815) 877-6777

Interpretive Exhibits, Inc., Bill Clark
1865 Beach Ave. NE, Salem, OR 97303
(503) 371-9411

Interpretive Graphics Signs & Systems, Jim Peters
3590 Summerhill Dr., Salt Lake City, UT 84121
(801) 942-5812
Examples on page 68.

KLB Exhibits, Wendy Smith
440 Short St., Missoula, MT 59801
(406) 721-5410

Kestrel Design Group
P.O. 910, Wheeling, IL 60090
(708) 520-0063

Pilley Associates, Tanner Pilley
4717 E. Brison del Sur, Tucson, AZ 85718-3602
(602) 299-3252
Examples on pages 11, 16, 17, 44.

Raymond Price Associates, Ray S. Price
P.O. Box 247, Fredrick, MD 21701
(301) 663-0995

Sycamore Associates, Jan Muir
P.O. Box 240, Trout Lake, WA 98650
(409) 395-2529

Terri Talas
P.O. Box 720, Newburyport, MA 01950
(508) 462-0202

Team Interpretation, Douglas Bruce McHenry
P.O. Box 429, Marston Mills, MA 02648
(508) 428-8924

John Veverka & Associates, John Veverka
P.O. Box 26095, Lansing, MI 48909
(517) 394-5355

Wilderness Graphics, Marvin Cook
P.O. Box 1635, Tallahassee, FL 32302
(904) 224-6414
Examples on page 25, 54; series on pages 63-66.

Clip Art
Creative ReSources, Inc.
P.O. Box 488, Flagstaff, AZ 86002
(602) 774-2147
Publisher of the "Interpretive Clip Art Library"

Fabricators

Metal Fabrication of Exhibit Bases and Hardware
Hopewell Manufacturing, Paul Kramer
Route 12, Box 272, Hagerstown, MD 21740
(301) 582-2343

Maps
Trails Illustrated, Mary Kay Stoehr, William L. Stoehr
P.O. Box 3610, Evergreen, CO 80439-3425
(800) 962-1643, (303) 670-3457

Vision Cartographics, Inc.
1925 Old Ranch Rd., Colorado Springs, CO 80908
(719) 598-9648

Carved Wood
Handcrafted Cedar Signs, Ron Zimmerman
Schmeeckle Reserve, UW-SP, Stevens Point, WI 54481
(715) 346-4992
Series on pages 57-61.

Sandblasted Wood
Cook & Company, Signmakers, Jude Cook
134 S. Tuscon Blvd.
Tuscon, AZ 85716-5517
(602) 622-2868

Interpretive Graphics Signs & Systems, Jim Peters
3590 Summerhill Dr., Salt Lake City, UT 84121
(801) 942-5812
Examples on page 68.

Wilderness Graphics, Marvin Cook
P.O. Box 1635, Tallahassee, FL 32302
(904) 224-6414
Example on page 62.

Metal Micro-Imaging
Interpretive Graphics Signs & Systems, Jim Peters
3590 Summerhill Dr., Salt Lake City, UT 84121
(801) 942-5812
Example on page 68.

Fiberglass Embedment
Pannier Graphics, John Fitch
Industrial Park, Warminster, PA 18974
(800) 544-8428, (215) 672-3600

Porcelain Enamel
ENAMELTEC, Jennifer Fairclough
60 Armstrong Ave., Georgetown, Ontario L7G 4R9
(800) 663-8543, (416) 873-1677

Fireform Porcelain, Inc., Scott McCallum
368 Yolanda Ave., Santa Rosa, CA 95404
(800) 643-3181, (707) 523-0580

Porcelain Company, David Berfield
9461 Mandus Olson Rd., Bainbridge Island, WA 98110
(206) 842-6210
Example page 17.

Winsor Porcelain Enamel Display, Jay R. Janny
311 Capitol Way North, Olympia, WA 98501
(206) 786-8200

Lexan/Aluminum Laminate
Genesis Graphics
1717 N. Lincoln Rd., Escanaba, MI 49829
(800) 659-7734, (906) 786-4913
Example on page 18.

Carsonite® Composite
Carsonite International
1301 Hot Springs Road
Carson City, NV 87906
(800) 648-7974, (702) 883-5104

Chromalin® Laminate
The Graphics Group, Florence Bramley, Director
P.O. Box 070216
Staten Island, NY 10307-0002
(718) 317-9800

Digital Sound Units
Tour Mate Systems Limited, Max N. Slivka
449 Adelaide St. W., Toronto, Ontario, Canada M5V 1T1
(416) 594-2376

AKMAN, Inc.
5767 Major Blvd., Orlando, FL 32819
(407) 351-1085

Promotional Technologies
5100 W. Silver Springs Blvd., Suite 700, Ocala, FL 32670
(904) 873-0758

See page 35 of this handbook for an example of a digital
sound repeater.

Ordering books in the Interpreter's Handbook Series	1-9 Copies	10-24 Copies	25+ Copies
Making the Right Connections: A Guide for Nature Writers	$7.50/copy	$6.00/copy	$5.00/copy
The Interpreter's Guidebook: Techniques for Programs and Presentations	$14.00/copy	$12.00/copy	$10.00/copy
Creating Environmental Publications: A Guide to Writing and Designing for Interpreters and Environmental Educators	$14.00/copy	$12.00/copy	$10.00/copy
Signs, Trails, and Wayside Exhibits: Connecting People and Places	$20.00/copy	$18.00/copy	$16.00/copy
Complete Series Set (4 books, one of each)	$45.50/set ($10 savings)		

Shipped postage paid in U.S. All others, shipping extra.

Make check payable to: College of Natural Resources, UWSP. Purchase orders accepted.
Mail to: Michael Gross, College of Natural Resources, UWSP, Stevens Point, WI 54481